Revised

New Children's Illustrated History

O.L. Henderson
Richard Ward

CLASS 4

OXFORD
UNIVERSITY PRESS

YMCA Library Building, Jai Singh Road, New Delhi 110001

Oxford University Press is a department of the University of Oxford.
It furthers the University's objective of excellence in research, scholarship,
and education by publishing worldwide in

Oxford New York
Auckland Cape Town Dar es Salaam Hong Kong Karachi
Kuala Lumpur Madrid Melbourne Mexico City Nairobi
New Delhi Shanghai Taipei Toronto

With offices in
Argentina Austria Brazil Chile Czech Republic France Greece
Guatemala Hungary Italy Japan Poland Portugal Singapore
South Korea Switzerland Thailand Turkey Ukraine Vietnam

Oxford is a registered trade mark of Oxford University Press
in the UK and in certain other countries.

Published in India
by Oxford University Press

First published as *A Children's Illustrated History*, 1977
Revised as *New Children's Illustrated History*, 1997
Third edition 2007
Ninth impression 2010

ISBN-13: 978-0-19-568385-1
ISBN-10: 0-19-568385-4

Illustrations by Kallol Majumder

Typeset in Aldine BT 401
by Bukprint, Delhi
Printed in India by Shiva Printech Pvt. Ltd., New Delhi 110039
and published by Oxford University Press
YMCA Library Building, Jai Singh Road, New Delhi 110001

Preface

There is general agreement among historians and history teachers in favour of creating a background of world history before children are introduced to the history of their own country. This gives students a sense of continuity when they study the history of their own people. This book is the first in a series of three books on world history for the Junior School. This preliminary course aims at introducing the child to the various phases of historical development beginning with the earliest civilizations.

This new edition has been thoroughly revised taking into account the feedback given by teachers. Many new elements have been added. The concept of **timelines** gives the children an idea of the time frame and brings events into perspective. Most of the chapters now have **maps** to give the children a sense of the geographical locations. **New topics and chapters** have been included to make it more current and up-to-date. **Did you knows** add interest. The activity section includes interactive and exciting **things to do** which will develop the children's interest in history.

This book for Class 3 begins with an introduction to history and concludes with the death of Julius Caesar. Class 4 begins with a chapter on Jesus Christ and takes the child up to the eighteenth century. In Class 5 the child is introduced to the American War of Independence and ends with the achievements of Nelson Mandela. The three books take the child from the past to the present. Each chapter is in the form of a story or a simple narrative told interestingly. Both biographical and culture-epoch methods have been used. The heroes of war and peace find their place in the former method while the latter approach highlights important historical events and processes. The chapters are arranged chronologically with timelines given at the beginning. The children are made aware of the development of writing, town planning, states, empires and religions. At all times the level of understanding displayed by the children in that particular age-group has been kept in mind.

The photographs and illustrations have been chosen, as far as possible, from contemporary or traditional sources rather than from fanciful reconstruction. Children are introduced to sources of history when they try to relate these materials to the findings of historians. The exercises reinforce learning. Word-notes at the beginning of each chapter draw attention to new ideas or concepts introduced in the chapter as well as to words that might be unfamiliar to the child.

Contents

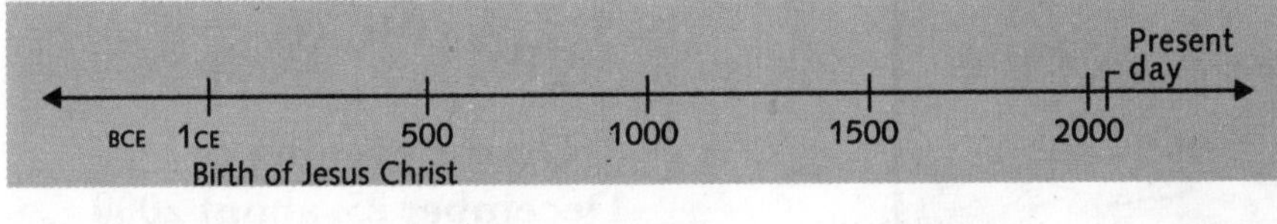

1

Jesus Christ

—The saviour

You will recall from your earlier book the letters BCE and CE after or before dates. These letters stand for *Before Common Era* and *Common Era.* The CE is the period of measured time beginning with the year 1 (the traditional birthdate of Jesus Christ) to the present. BCE or Before Common Era is connected to dates before 1 CE.

Some examples of dates are as follows:

Julius Caesar was born in	100 BCE
Hannibal died in	183 BCE
Akbar died in	1605 CE
Mahatma Gandhi died in	1948 CE

As you can see, all these dates are counted from the birth of Christ, although people are not sure when Christ was born. In this chapter we will read about Jesus Christ.

Jesus was born in a country called Palestine on the Mediterranean coast. The people of Palestine were followers of Judaism or members of the Jewish community. At that time, the Romans were ruling over Palestine. The Jews had their own officials,

Words to remember

scriptures : the holy writings of a religion.

disciples : followers of any leader of religious thought.

resurrection : to return to life again after death.

literally : exactly; word for word.

authorities : (here) rulers.

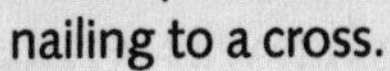

crucified : put to death by nailing to a cross.

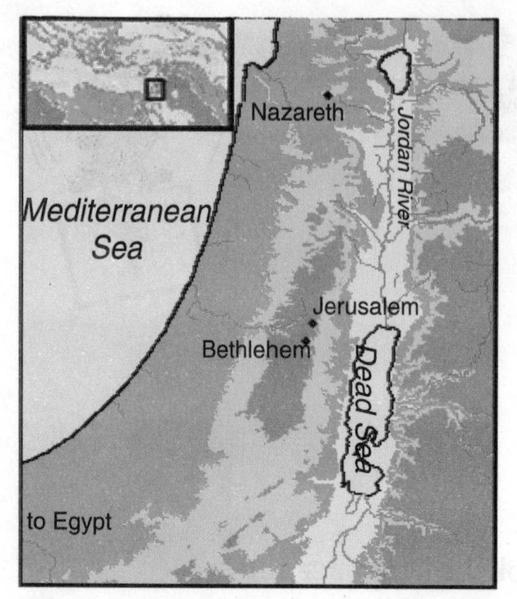

Places connected with Jesus Christ's birth

Did you know?

On the evening of December 25, about 2000 years ago, Mary delivered baby Jesus in a stable. Soon afterwards, he was visited by angels, shepherds and wise men from the east known as the Magi.

but the man in charge was the Governor who took his orders from Rome. Jesus was born in a tiny village called Bethlehem in the family of a carpenter named Joseph. He grew up in a place called Nazareth, near the lake of Galilee in North Palestine. As soon as Jesus was old enough, he started to work with Joseph in the carpentry shop. His mother, Mary, brought him up to be a good Jew and taught him the Jewish **scriptures**.

Jesus was born in Bethlehem

As Jesus grew up, he became more and more thoughtful. He could see that people were not happy. He noticed a great difference between the rich and the poor. He saw that many rich Jews did not follow what was written in the scriptures.

When Jesus was about thirty years old, he started to go around the country preaching to people and asking them to change their evil ways. He told them that they should be kind and thoughtful and help each other in times of need. A number of people, many of them very poor, listened to what he said and believed in him. They became his **disciples**, that is, people who accompanied him and helped in his work.

Jesus wanted people to live together in peace

The things which Jesus taught were not liked by everybody. The Jews did not like him because he criticized the Jewish priests for following the scriptures too **literally**. The Jews had many rules, and sometimes these rules were cruel. When Jesus talked to the Jews about this they became very angry and ordered him to stop his preaching. When Jesus disobeyed them and continued with his teaching and preaching, he made many enemies. The Jews then decided to punish him very severely for this.

Jesus entering Jerusalem for the Passover

The Jews held a great feast each year called the **Passover**. It was a very important feast, especially in Jerusalem, and the whole city was filled with people. They came from every part of the country to celebrate the Passover. Jesus knew that he had many enemies amongst the Jews, but he was not afraid. He went to Jerusalem at the time of the Passover to preach to the people.

Jesus had often told his followers that God, his father would come again to the world to gather together, only the good and the righteous and set up his new kingdom known as the Kingdom of God. The wicked people would be left out and punished. When the Jewish priests heard these words, they attacked Jesus and reported him to the Roman **authorities**. Jesus was brought to trial before the Roman Governor, Pontius Pilate. But he was found innocent.

The Crucifixion

You can imagine how angry his enemies were. They shouted at Pilate in anger and demanded that Jesus be crucified. However, the Roman Governor Pontius Pilate thought that it was really not fair to give him such a severe punishment, but when the angry crowd kept shouting, 'Crucify him! Crucify him!', he took some water and washed his hands in front of them to make it clear to one and all, that he did not want to be associated with Jesus' punishment. He asked the Jews to decide amongst themselves as to what punishment they wished to give Jesus. So the Jews took charge of Jesus. There on that Friday afternoon, they nailed him to the cross. Jesus remained nailed to the cross until he died. He was then only thirty three years old!

In spite of all the cruel treatment meted out to him by his enemies, his last words of prayer on the cross were, 'Father forgive them, for they know not what they are doing.'

His family and friends then took his body down from the cross, wrapped it in a white cloth and laid it in a tomb in the garden near by. They rolled a big stone at the opening of the tomb to seal it. On the third day, that is on Sunday morning, when his disciples and friends, did not find his body in the tomb, they were both surprised and very sad. Jesus then appeared to them and told them that he had been raised to life by God, his father and was being taken up to heaven to live with him.

Each year, Christians all over the world mourn the death of Jesus Christ on Good Friday and celebrate his resurrection on Easter Sunday.

Jesus did not write down any of his teachings, but four of his disciples wrote accounts of his life and teachings. They not only wrote an account of what he had taught but they also continued his work. They went around the country telling people to follow the word of Christ. The writings of these four disciples were later known as the **Gospels**. The Gospels and the writings of all the Prophets before the birth of Christ are all compiled in one book known as the *Bible*. The *Bible* is the most holy and sacred book of the Christians.

Jesus is called the Saviour because he taught people how to lead a good and useful life. This would help them to overcome their miseries and be happy. He showed people how each one of them could overcome the evils of the world if they wanted to. He often told them simple and interesting stories to illustrate his teachings. These stories are known as **Parables**. He wanted people to love God, to look after their parents and to be kind to everyone. He wanted them to look after the sick and the poor, to obey the laws and not to be selfish. He asked men not to seek high positions in the world, but to be humble.

After the death of Jesus, his disciples faced great difficulties. Some years after Jesus's death, a Jew called Saul, who was a Roman citizen, began to attack the disciples of Jesus. One day, however, when he was on his way to the city of Damascus, a strange thing happened. He suddenly saw a great flash of light and fell down on the ground. Then he heard a voice call out to him, 'Saul! Saul! Why do you attack my disciples?'

From that moment Saul became a disciple of Jesus. He changed his name to Paul and went to many countries spreading the teachings of Jesus. This was the beginning of the Christian faith which later spread to all parts of the world. Today, even people who do not belong to this faith celebrate Christmas, a popular festival that marks the birth of Jesus Christ.

Exercises

1. **Answer the following.**
   (a) What do the letters CE and BCE mean?
   (b) Why did the Jews become angry with Jesus?
   (c) What were the teachings of Jesus?
   (d) Why is Jesus called the Saviour?
   (e) Why did Pontius Pilate wash his hands before the people?

2. **Fill in the blanks.**
   (a) Jesus was born in a village called .... but grew up in a place called ....
   (b) Jesus's mother was ....; she brought him up to be a good ....
   (c) Every year the Jews held a great feast called the ....
   (d) The Roman Governor called .... tried Jesus.
   (e) The writings of the four disciples were known as ....

3. **Say whether the following are True or False.**
   (a) Jesus was the son of a doctor named Joseph.
   (b) The things which Jesus taught were liked by everybody.
   (c) Jesus attacked many old customs of the Jews.
   (d) Christians celebrate both Christmas and Easter very joyously.
   (e) Saul changed his name to Paul and went to many countries spreading the teachings of Jesus.

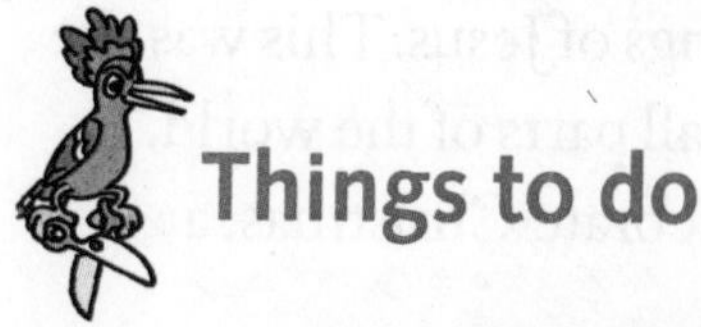

Things to do

1. **Design a card.**
   Make a Christmas card. You may draw or stick pictures on it.

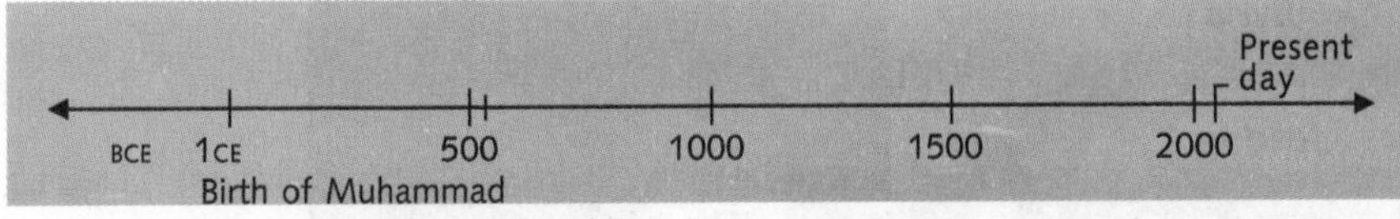

2

Muhammad

—The Prophet of Islam

About five hundred and seventy years after the birth of Jesus, another great **prophet** named Muhammad was born in a town called Mecca in Central Arabia. He later became the founder of Islam and the followers of his religion are called Muslims.

In those days, the Arabs worshipped a number of gods and some of their gods were natural things, such as trees and stones. In the centre of Mecca was a great black stone called Kaaba, which the Arabs thought was extremely holy. People of the Quraysh tribe looked after the stone and guarded it from any harm.

The Kaaba

Words to remember

prophet : person who teaches religion and is or claims to be inspired by God.

caravan : a group of people (vehicles or animals) making a journey together for safety, usually across the desert.

angel : a messenger of God.

idol : an image of a god, often carved in stone or wood and used as an object of worship.

mosque : a building in which Muslims worship.

pilgrimage : a journey to a holy place for religious reasons.

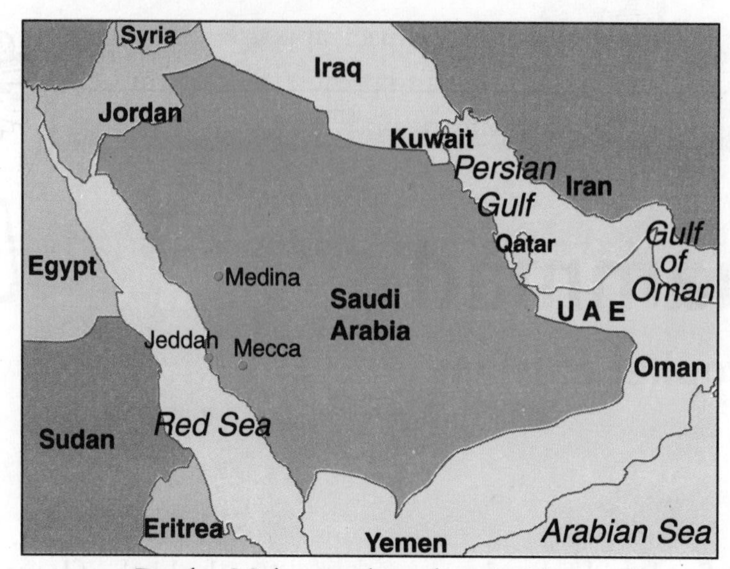

Prophet Muhammad was born in Mecca

Muhammad's family were members of the Quraysh tribe of Arabs. Muhammad's father, Abdullah, had died before he was born, and his mother, Aminah, died six years later. Muhammad was brought up by an uncle. He often travelled with his uncle on trading journeys to Syria.

There were always **caravans** of camels going across the desert for trade. These camels carried goods of every kind. Muhammad was a bright boy, and he soon found some work with the camel drivers and merchants. On one such journey, he was in charge of the goods of a rich woman called Khadijah. When he was twenty-five years old, Muhammad married Khadijah.

Muhammad and Khadijah had two sons, who died at a young age, and four daughters. Muhammad was very successful in his business but slowly he began to lose interest in it. He became very thoughtful and fond of being by himself. Sometimes he used to go to caves in the mountains to pray and think. On his journeys he had met Jews and Christians, and he often thought about the differences between religions. He spent most of his time thinking about God and at last, when he was forty, he decided to stop working at his business and to spend his time in thinking about which religion believed in true God. He wanted to convey his thoughts to other people.

It is said that one night an **angel**, Gabriel, appeared to him and said, 'O you who are covered with a cloak! Go and preach the word of God to everyone. Praise the Lord and keep away from sin.'

And so Muhammad gave up his work and went about preaching the word of God to all who would listen to him. Khadijah was the first to believe in his message. She also encouraged him in his work of preaching. Muhammad told the Arabs to throw away their idols and to worship one true God. Slowly he gathered some disciples round him. When Abu Bakr, an important man, joined the movement, it became very strong. But Muhammad had many enemies because the Arabs did not like his attacks on their **idols**. They said the idols were gods; Muhammad said there was only one God. The Arabs said that their people were the greatest in the world. Muhammad said that all men everywhere were equal, that no one was greater than the other. The Arabs also thought that when a man died, that was the end of him. Muhammad told people that there was another life after death and that those who lived bad lives would be punished.

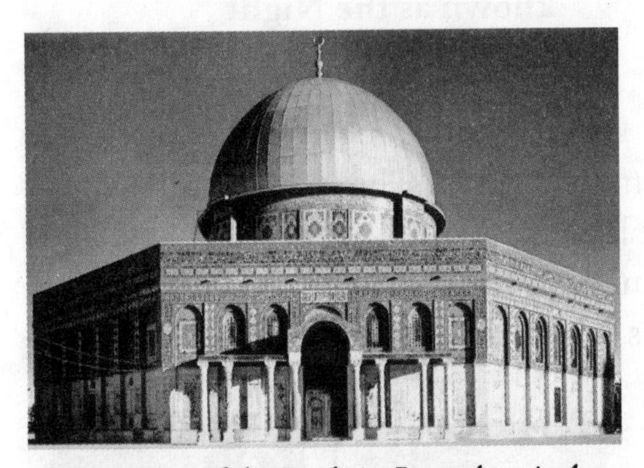

The Dome of the Rock in Jerusalem is the first monument of Islam

These ideas made many people in Mecca very angry, and some of the Arabs joined together and decided to kill Muhammad. They met one night in a house in Mecca to carry out their plan that very night. But in the middle of the night, the angel Gabriel warned Muhammad not to sleep in his usual bed. In this way, Muhammad escaped from being murdered. The next morning he went to the house of Abu Bakr and told him that he was leaving Mecca. 'I am full of joy,' said Abu Bakr. 'I was waiting for this moment. I have two camels ready.' The two men then made their way to a cave in a mountain near Mecca where they hid themselves for three days.

The men of the Quraysh tribe were furious when they found that Muhammad had escaped. They offered a reward of one hundred camels to anybody who could capture him. After three days Abu Bakr and Muhammad rode away on their camels to a place called Medina.

Did you know?

One night, the angel Gabriel woke Muhammad and took him on a journey to Jerusalem. That is where he heard Allah's instructions that Muslims should pray five times a day. This is known as the Night Journey.

At last Muhammad reached Medina. The journey from Mecca to Medina is called the *Hegira* (*hijrah*) or migration; it took place in 622 CE. It is from this year that the Muslims count the years, and not from the birth of Christ. Muhammad lived in Medina for a few years where he had a large number of followers. When they were strong enough, he and his men attacked Mecca. They soon conquered the city and broke all the idols except the black stone. Muhammad then returned to Medina.

Muhammad slowly got the Arabs to believe in his teachings. Over the years, the Arabs became united, and slowly became one state. Muhammad died in 632 CE. The teachings of Muhammad were later written down by his followers in a book called the *Koran*.

A page from the holy Koran

The *Koran* tells Muslims to follow a few simple rules. First, they should believe that there is only one God and that Muhammad is his Prophet. They should say regular prayers facing Mecca and they should also say prayers together on Fridays in the **mosque**, to show that all men are equal. They should give money to the poor. Every year, in the holy month of Ramzan, they should take no food or drink during the hours of daylight. If possible, they should make a **pilgrimage** to Mecca.

Islam has spread to many parts of the world and has influenced many people.

Exercises

1. **Answer the following.**
   - (a) What did the angel Gabriel tell Muhammad when she appeared to him for the first time?
   - (b) Why did the Arabs want to kill Muhammad?
   - (c) Which is the most important date in the Muslim calendar? Why?
   - (d) Who was Abu Bakr?
   - (e) What are the few rules that Muslims should follow?

2. **Match the following.**

(a) Ramzan	Helped Muhammad
(b) Khadijah	Muhammad's journey from Mecca to Medina
(c) Abu Bakr	Wife of Muhammad
(d) Hegira	Holy month

3. **Say whether the following are True or False.**
   - (a) Muhammad was the founder of Islam and his followers came to be called Muslims.
   - (b) Muhammad wanted his followers to worship idols.
   - (c) The Muslims count the years from the birth of the Christ.
   - (d) The Muslims say prayers together on Fridays in the mosque, to show that all men are equal.

Things to do

1. **For your scrapbook**
   Find out about a mosque in your city. Write five sentences about it.

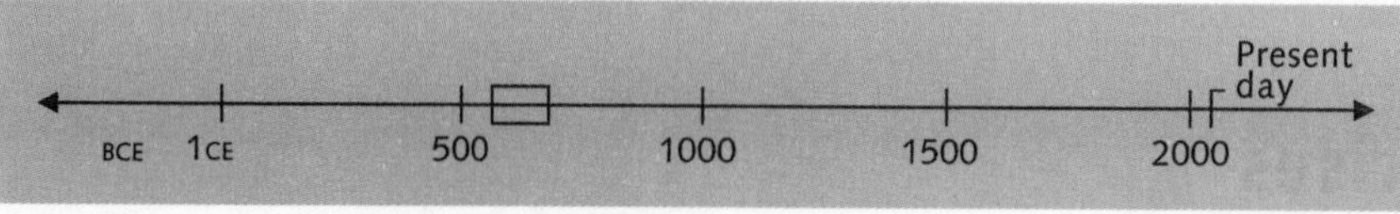

King Harsha
—A kind ruler

About six hundreds years after the birth of Christ, there was a king called Prabhakaravardhana at Thanesar in East Punjab. The king had two sons. The elder son was called Rajyavardhana, and the younger one was called Harshavardhana. King Prabhakaravardhana gave his daughter, Rajyasri, in marriage to the king of Kanauj.

The kings in those days were always fighting with one another and each one wanted his kingdom to be the largest. When Prabhakaravardhana died, Rajyavardhana was made king in his place. The king of Malwa, called Deva Gupta, wanted to capture the kingdom of Kanauj. He sent his men to kill the king of Kanauj, and when they had killed him they carried off his wife, Rajyasri.

Rajyavardhana died while **avenging** his brother-in-law's death. The chief minister of Thanesar immediately sent for Harsha and asked him to be the king. When the **statesmen** of Kanauj offered the crown to Harsha, he hesitated.

'I do not know,' he said, 'whether I shall make a good king or not. A king should rule wisely and I do not know whether I can do that.'

Words to remember

avenging : taking revenge for.
statesmen : people who play an important part in the management of state affairs, especially those who are skilled and experienced.
withered : dried up.
prosperous : rich and successful.

However, Harsha soon found himself at the head of the kingdom of his brother as well as that of his brother-in-law. He made Kanauj his capital.

When he came to the throne Harsha had to face many problems. He was very angry that his sister had been carried away by Deva Gupta and he wanted to find her. Rajyasri had been thrown into a dark prison at Kanauj. After many weeks, she managed to escape. She left the fortress and walked on and on alone into the hills and forests of Malwa. For some days, she managed to live on fruits from the trees and water from the streams. But slowly, day by day, she got weaker and weaker.

One evening, just as the sun was setting, she came to a rocky hillside. She had been walking all day and she was nearly fainting. She found an old, **withered** tree in front of her. She sat down and started to cry.

'My dear husband has been killed,' she cried, 'and I have no one to look after me. I cannot go into the forest again. Death is the only thing left for me.'

She decided to kill herself.

'There is plenty of old wood here,' she thought. 'If only I had a fire I could light these sticks and finish my life in the flames.'

At that moment she heard the sound of galloping horses. Looking up, she could hardly believe her eyes. There was her brother Harsha! With horses and soldiers and a horse for her, too. He had come just in time.

For the next six years, Harsha attacked all the kings of northern India. His kingdom stretched from the west coast of Gujarat right across Central India to the east coast. He also wanted to conquer the kingdom of the Chalukyas in the South. The Chalukya king was called Pulakesin II. Pulakesin had good troops and elephants and he beat back all the attacks which Harsha made.

Now that Harsha had such a vast kingdom, he stopped his wars and became a just and kind ruler. He worked hard to make all the people in his kingdom happy and **prosperous**.

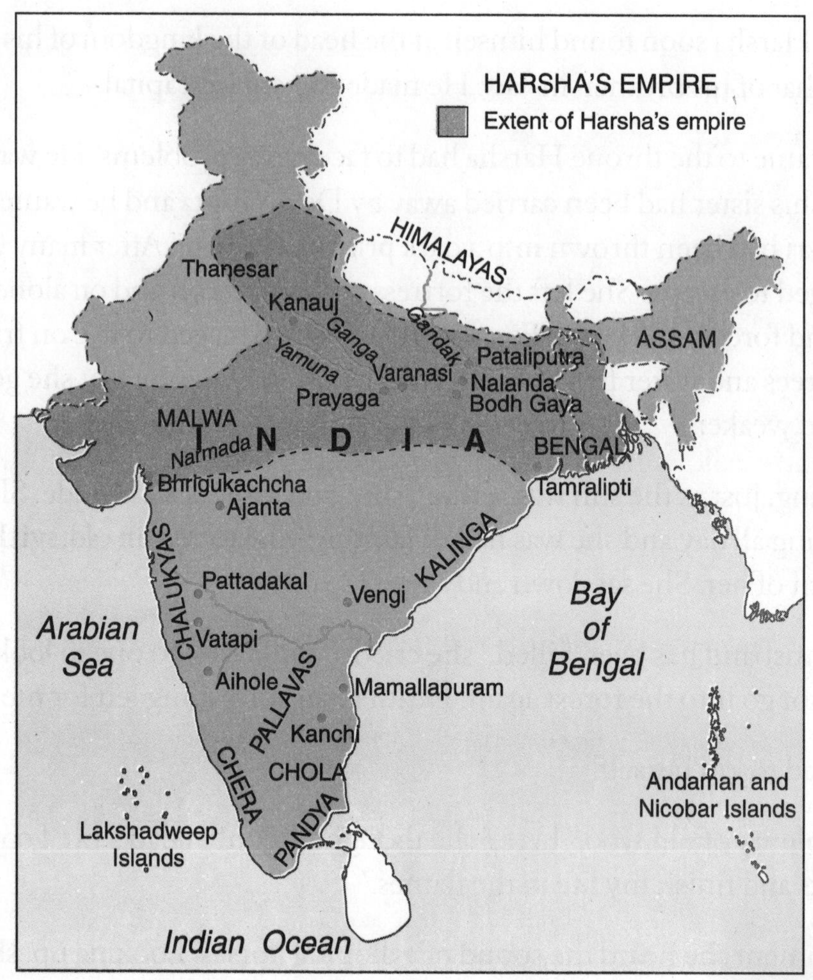

We know a great deal about the kingdom of Harsha from the writings of a famous Chinese traveller called Hiuen Tsang. Hiuen Tsang came overland from China and spent many years in Harsha's kingdom. When he was on his way to India, he received an invitation from Kumara, the king of Assam. Although he was a king, Kumara was also under the rule of Harsha. Harsha was at that time staying in Patna. When he heard that Kumara had invited Hiuen Tsang, Harsha got very angry. He sent a letter to Kumara telling him to send the Chinese guest to him at once.

Hiuen Tsang

'Hiuen Tsang is an important guest from China. He should visit me first, not you. You have done wrong in inviting him to your kingdom. Please send the honoured guest here immediately.'

Kumara wanted to keep Hiuen Tsang at his court for some weeks, and so he wrote to King Harsha:

'O Great King Harsha! The Chinese visitor is very dear to me. He is teaching us the word of the Buddha, and I beg you to allow him to stay here. I would prefer to send you my head on a gold plate rather than lose such a guest.'

Did you know?

Banabhatta the famous Indian writer, wrote *Harshacharita*, an account of the life and times of Harsha. It is one of the most important sources of information for the period.

Harsha's letter in reply was short:

'Yes, please send your head on a gold plate.'

Kumara was not as brave as he wanted Harsha to believe and he immediately sent Hiuen Tsang, with a big army and elephants and soldiers, to Harsha's court in Patna.

Harsha receiving Hiuen Tsang

During Harsha's time the most important university was at Nalanda. It is said that there were ten thousand students who were taught free. The money for running the university came from donations made by kings and rich people and taxes collected from about a hundred villages. The students were taught literature, logic, grammar, medicine and astronomy. Nalanda became so famous that students came even from other countries to study.

Ruins of Nalanda

Hiuen Tsang spent twenty-eight years in India and wrote a lengthy book about our country. We have this book even today. He tells us all about Harsha's kingdom and about his just and kind rule.

The Buddhist Council was very successful

Harsha arranged for a great meeting of holy men from all parts of the country at Kanauj. He wanted them to meet Hiuen Tsang and listen to him talk about Buddhism. When Hiuen Tsang gave his lectures, many of the people did not like what he said. Some of them joined together and wanted to kill him. Luckily Harsha's spies discovered the plot and told the king about it. Harsha became very angry. He sent out a warning to everybody that if anyone caused any harm to the holy visitor, he would be punished. The great meeting of the Buddhist Council went on for many days and many people talked about the teachings of the Buddha.

This first meeting was so successful that Harsha arranged for another one. This second meeting was held at Prayag, nowadays known as Allahabad. Prayag was a city which was built just where the river Yamuna joins the river Ganga. Many people came to that meeting. There were not only holy men from all religions, but also priests and philosophers; there were also many poor people. King Harsha gave rich presents to everybody who attended the meeting. There is a story which says that he went on giving presents until he had nothing left. When all his jewels, silver and gold had been given away, there were still two old men left who had not received any presents yet. King Harsha took off some of the rich clothes he was wearing and gave them as presents to the old men.

King Harsha died in 647 CE. Unfortunately he had no sons, and soon after his death there was much fighting for his kingdom and it was divided into small states.

Exercises

1. **Answer the following.**
   - (a) How did Harsha become the ruler of both Thanesar and Kanauj?
   - (b) Who was Hiuen Tsang?
   - (c) Why is the book written by Hiuen Tsang important in history?
   - (d) Describe the second great meeting that Harsha held.
   - (e) What happened to Harsha's kingdom after his death?

2. **Fill in the blanks.**
   - (a) Harsha was the son of king .... of Thanesar.
   - (b) Harsha made .... his capital.
   - (c) .... beat back all the attacks which Harsha made to conquer the kingdom of the Chalukyas.

(d) Hiuen Tsang spent .... years in India.

(e) The two great meetings were held at .... and ....

3. **Choose the correct answer.**

(a) King Prabhakaravardhana gave his daughter, Rajyasri, in marriage to the King of ....

i) Kanauj ii) Malwa iii) Assam iv) Gujarat

(b) Pulakesin II was a king of............

i) Northern India ii) Western India iii) Southern India iv) Central India

(c) Hiuen Tsang was a famous............. traveller.

i) Indian ii) Japanese iii) Chinese iv) American

(d) Hiuen Tsang was a follower of ....

i) Islam ii) Buddhism iii) Jainism iv) Christianity

(e) Harsha was a .... ruler.

i) cruel ii) coward iii) wicked iv) just and kind

Things to do

1. **For your scrapbook.**

Find out the location of Nalanda. Collect pictures and write ten sentences about it in your scrapbook.

2. **Map work.**

Look at the map of Asia and try to locate China.

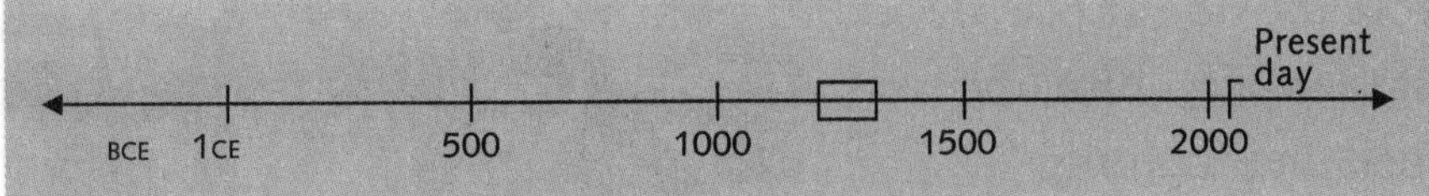

4

Marco Polo

—An Italian traveller in China

From very early times, Central Asia has been the home of many **nomadic tribes**. These tribes would wander from place to place seeking water and food for their cattle and sheep. The Mongols were one such tribe. Wherever they went they carried their belongings. These were guarded by the Mongol men on horseback. Hundreds of years of this kind of life had made the Mongols excellent horsemen and fierce fighters. Occasionally, one leader would rise and the Mongols would become powerful, and dangerous to other people living in neighbouring countries like India, China and

The Mongols were excellent horsemen

Words to remember

nomadic tribes : groups of people roaming from place to place in search of fresh pastures.
monks : members of a religious community of men living under certain vows.
monastery : building in which monks live as a community.
disappointment : failure to get what is hoped for.
harbour : place of shelter for ships.
wreck : to damage a ship so much that it sinks or can no longer sail.
Genoese : people of Genoa.

Afghanistan. Before the rule of Harsha and even hundreds of years after him, the Mongols continued their fighting.

Chengiz Khan

About 1200 CE, the Mongols had a strong ruler called Chengiz Khan. Chengiz Khan made friends with some people called Tartars, and together they attacked China and captured Peking. They then invaded Persia, Afghanistan and Russia. You can find all these places on the map on page 25. Chengiz Khan then ruled over a huge empire. He was not only a brave soldier but also an able ruler. The later Khans made the empire even bigger and captured Baghdad. At last, in 1260 CE, the most famous of the Khans came to the throne: his name was Kublai Khan. Before he came to the throne, he moved the capital of his kingdom to Peking. He lived in a magnificent palace and ruled his vast kingdom wisely.

Kublai Khan

Now at that time Venice, in Italy, was a great trading centre. Merchants came there from all parts of the world, and brought back pearls and silk cloth and other things from the Far East. In Venice, there were two merchants called Nicolo and Maffeo Polo. One day they set out for Constantinople. From there they went on to Bokhara. In Bokhara, they bought fine rugs and carpets and decided to return to Venice. They were sitting one night in the resting place for travellers when some Persians appeared. They began to talk to them.

'Where are you from?' they asked the Persians, 'It looks as though you have come from Persia.'

'We have,' replied the men.

'And are you not returning to Persia?' asked Nicolo.

'No indeed we are not,' replied the Persians. 'We are going to Peking, in China, to visit the great king, Kublai Khan.'

'Quite a long way, I have heard,' said Nicolo, 'and you will have to cross the vast Gobi Desert. What will you find there? Why are you going?'

'We shall find silk,' said the Persians. 'Chinese silk is the most beautiful in the world.'

Nicolo and Maffeo talked far into the night and in the morning they asked the Persians if they could join them. The next day they set out on their long journey. After many months they finally arrived at the court of Kublai Khan.

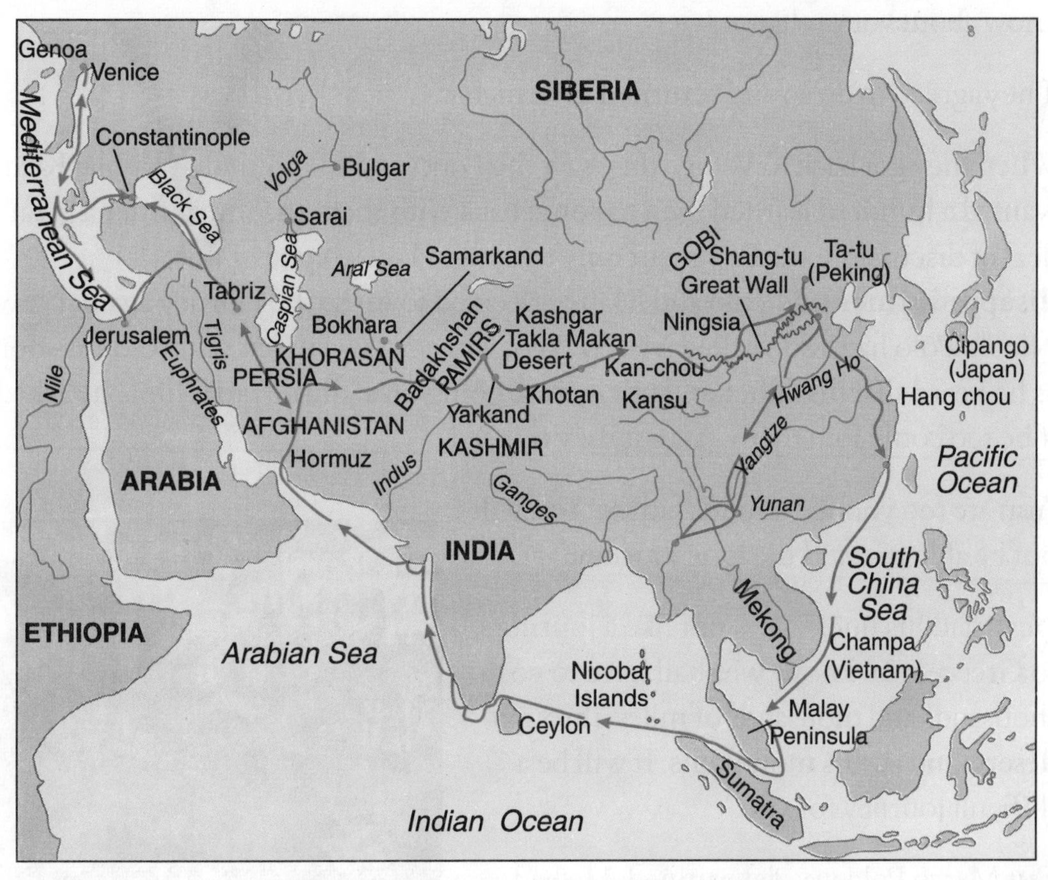

How Marco Polo travelled to China and back

Kublai Khan was a Buddhist, but he was also very interested in other religions. He welcomed Nicolo and Maffeo from Venice and soon began to talk to them about their religion.

'I should like to learn all about Christianity, but who is here to teach me? You have come for business and know little about your religion.' 'Yes,' said Nicolo. 'And you have been kind enough to give us silk; we shall take it back to Venice and sell it at a great price. What can we do in return?'

'I have an idea,' said the Khan suddenly. 'You can bring a hundred men who know about your religion. A hundred **monks** from one of your **monasteries**. Then I can send them out to all parts of my kingdom so that everyone will know about your religion.'

They agreed to do so and returned to Venice.

When they got back to Venice they saw the Pope, and told him that Kublai Khan wanted a hundred learned men to come back with them to China. After a great deal of discussion, the Pope sent only two men. But in spite of this **disappointment**, Nicolo and Maffeo decided to make the journey again. Now Nicolo Polo had a son called Marco Polo, who was seventeen years old. As soon as he heard that his father and uncle were going on a journey to China, he asked if he too could join them. At first they refused.

'You are too young,' said his father. 'You will not be able to stand the long journey.'

'Yes,' said his uncle. 'It is not like a journey to Greece, you know. We shall have to go thousands and thousands of miles, through deserts and across mountains. It will be a difficult journey for you.'

But Marco Polo was determined. He had been listening to stories of China and

Marco Polo leaving Venice

Kublai Khan from his father and uncle for the last two years. He would very often try to imagine Kublai Khan's palace and the Chinese gardens and the long caravans of camels and mules, and he did his best to persuade his father and uncle to take him along with them. At last they agreed and in 1271 CE, they all set out on their journey. The two learned men refused to join them. It was good that they took young Marco with them, for, many years later, he wrote down everything he had seen and heard in China in a famous book called *The Travels of Marco Polo, the Venetian.*

The Polo brothers wanted to go most of the way by sea. They went from Venice to Persia and then went down to the mouth of the Persian Gulf, to a place called Hormuz. There they hoped to get a ship which would take them to China. But when they saw the ships in the **harbour** which would take them to China, they were frightened. The boats were small sailing ships made without any nails. The planks of the ships were sewn together with a string. They had only one sail and were often **wrecked** in the strong winds.

The Polos decided to go back 200 miles or more, and go by land to China. They travelled on camels. Day after day they walked through the desert. There were no animals or birds, there were no trees, there was no water. They had to carry everything with them on their camels. At last they left the desert and started climbing up the mountains. Finally they arrived in Kashmir. There the scenery changed as there were trees, flowers and beautiful lakes and streams. But they went on and on, and after crossing the great Gobi Desert, they eventually reached the Great Wall of China.

Marco Polo with his father and uncle

Once they entered China, the news of their arrival soon

reached Kublai Khan. He was a very efficient ruler and could receive messages from every part of his kingdom within a very short time. At every small town, he had a man with a pony. When a message was to be sent, the man set off on his pony and after he had gone twenty miles, he handed over the message to another man, who went another twenty miles. In this way any message which was sent could reach Kublai Khan very quickly.

Did you know?

Marco Polo was one of the first Europeans to visit China.

Kublai Khan was very happy to see the Polo brothers again, although he was disappointed that they had not brought any learned men with them. The whole journey had taken them more than three years and Marco Polo was now twenty-one years old. The Khan was delighted to see him and welcomed him to his palace. What a wonderful palace it was! The walls were decorated with beautiful cloth of silk with gold embroidery, there were magnificent statues and marble floors, and the palace was surrounded by gardens and fountains.

Marco Polo at the court of Kublai Khan

Kublai Khan was very pleased with Marco Polo and he asked him to take up a post in his service. Marco Polo set to work, and as he was hard working and honest, he did well and was very successful. The Khan sent him to all parts of his kingdom, and he even went to Ceylon. The Khan wanted to buy a tooth of the Buddha and sent Marco on this strange journey.

Marco Polo wrote down all these adventures in his book, giving many descriptions of the countries he visited. He was amazed at the capital city, Peking, where the Emperor lived. There was a great wall round the city and there were many gates. At each gate there was a tall tower and in this tower lived a thousand soldiers who guarded this gate. In the centre of the city, there was another tower with a huge bell at the top. When the bell was rung at night, the people of Peking knew that it was time to go home. Nobody was allowed in the streets after the bell had rung.

Marco Polo served Kublai Khan faithfully for seventeen years. The Khan was growing old, and although Marco Polo had worked well, he was afraid that when the Khan died, he might be attacked by those people who had been jealous of him. He wanted to return to Venice. Luckily, a Chinese princess wanted to go to Persia, where she was going to marry the ruler of Persia who was the grandnephew of the Khan. The Polos offered to accompany and take her safely to Persia. Kublai Khan was unwilling to let them go but finally granted permission. They set off by sea and went to Ceylon, from there to South India, and then up to the Persian Gulf. When they reached Persia, they heard that Kublai Khan had died and so they decided not to go back to China.

When they arrived in Venice in 1295 CE, they had changed so much that their friends and relations did not recognize them. Worse still, when they started telling stories about the things that they had seen, nobody believed them. It was only when those around saw jewels and precious stones pouring from the sleeves of the thick Chinese coats they were wearing, that they began to believe the stories!

A portrait of Marco Polo

A year later Marco Polo was taken prisoner by the **Genoese**—great rivals of the Venetians at sea—during a sea battle. While he was in prison he found a man who could write well and Marco began to dictate his tale. These stories turned into a famous book. Fortunately, he was soon released from prison and lived happily in Venice for many years. His stories of China became stranger and stranger and his friends in Venice called him *Marco*

Millioni, which means in Italian, *Marco the Million Man,* because all his stories were about millions and millions of precious stones!

Exercises

1. Answer the following.

(a) Who was Chengiz Khan?

(b) From whom did the Polos hear about Kublai Khan?

(c) Why did they go to China the second time even though the journey from Venice to Peking was both long and dangerous?

(d) Who was Marco Polo? Why was Kublai Khan pleased with him?

(e) What did Marco Polo write in his book, *The Travels of Marco Polo, the Venetian?*

2. Say whether the following are True or False.

(a) Venice was a great trading centre.

(b) The Polos visited the court of Chengiz Khan, who was the ruler of China.

(c) Kublai Khan was a Buddhist.

(d) Kublai Khan was not happy to see the Polos.

(e) The great desert the Polos crossed before they reached the Great Wall of China is called Gobi Desert.

3. Match the following.

(a) Kublai Khan	Served Kublai Khan for seventeen years
(b) Marco Polo	The name given to Marco Polo by his friends
(c) Nicolo Polo	Moved the capital to Peking
(d) *Marco Millioni*	Father of Marco Polo

Things to do

1. **For your scrapbook.**
   Collect pictures of Chinese pots, silks and paintings.

2. **Map work.**
   On a world map mark Marco's route to China and back.

3. **Printing was invented in China. You can also try printing with vegetables.**

   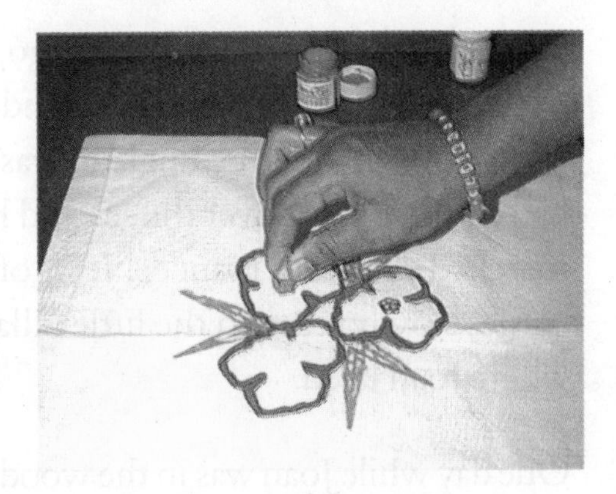

   You need: capsicum; ladies finger; fabric paint; brush; a knife; cloth
   Method: Take one capsicum and cut it into two pieces. Apply fabric paint of your choice carefully on the brim of the capsicum piece. Take care not to smudge. Punch the painted capsicum on the cloth to make petals of a flower. Cut the ladies finger lengthwise to make leaves and breadthwise to make small flower designs. Punch with the small flower design in the centre of the flowers. See the picture.

4. **Check out this website for some additional information.**
   http://www.bbc.co.uk/history/historic_figures/polo_marco.shtml (accessed on 14 August 2006)

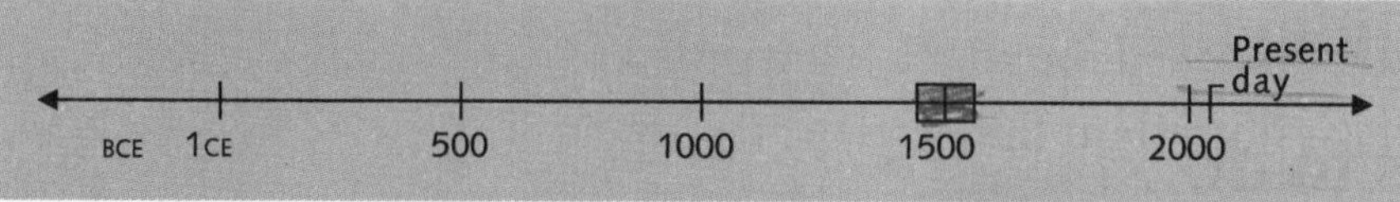

5

Joan of Arc

—The girl who saved France

More than 500 years ago, a girl called Joan was born in France. Her father and mother were simple farmers. At that time, England was at war with France. The English soldiers had come in ships over the sea and had beaten some of the French armies and marched deep into France. News of the battles slowly reached the little village where Joan lived.

One day while Joan was in the woods, she knelt down to say her prayers. Suddenly she heard a voice. It was the voice of an angel. The angel said:

'Get up, brave girl—your time has come, you have to go to King Charles of France. Tell him that you will be a general in his army and that you will drive the English out of France.'

Joan was afraid.

Words to remember

captain : leader or chief commander.

studded : thickly set.

armour : a protective covering for the body, usually of metal, worn when fighting.

banner : a flag on a pole used as the standard of a king, knight, etc. especially in battle.

witch : a woman thought to have evil magic powers.

saint : holy person; one who is declared by the Church to have won a high place in heaven.

'How can I do that?' she asked the angel. 'I am only a girl of seventeen. I cannot ride at the head of an army and fight the enemy. Even if I do, who would listen to a girl like me?'

Joan of Arc

Then the angel said, 'Do not be afraid, you will have to be brave and you will have to believe in God.'

Joan went back to her village and told her story. Everybody laughed at her, but she decided to go and see the **captain**, the most important officer of the army in her district. She put on her best clothes and went off to see him. When she got there, she found a sentry at the gate.

'I have come to see the captain,' said Joan. 'I have very important business with him.'

'Get out!' said the sentry. 'You can't come in here. The captain is busy. In any case, he certainly does not want to see a village girl like you. Go home.'

'I shall not go home,' said Joan. 'I shall sit here on this stone until you let me in.'

The sentry smiled. 'You can sit there for a week, if you like,' he said, 'but you are not going to see the captain.'

'I shall see,' said Joan. She sat on a stone opposite the sentry and looked straight at him. After half an hour the sentry began to feel uncomfortable. The sentry looked at Joan, and then he saw a strange light in her eyes. He began to feel frightened.

'I'm going to see the captain,' said Joan and pushed her way past the sentry. She started climbing the steps. The steps were of stone and the staircase was dark. When she started climbing the stairs she felt quite brave, but when she got to the top and looked down the long dark corridor, she trembled a little and felt frightened; but she soon remembered what the angel had told her. So she marched bravely down the corridor and knocked on a great iron door **studded** with black nails. She could hear the voices of some men inside as she pushed open the door. Five men were seated at the table drinking wine. Joan marched into the room.

'Which of you is the captain?'

The captain, who was sitting at the head of the table, was too surprised to speak. He wondered how a young girl had pushed her way past the sentry.

'I have received orders from an angel in Heaven,' said Joan. 'He told me to come to you for help; I need a sword and a horse and then I can go to King Charles and help him drive the English out of our country.'

The captain was an old soldier and had fought many battles, but when he looked into Joan's eyes and heard her brave words, he suddenly felt frightened.

'Come along,' commanded Joan, 'I need these things immediately.'

The captain looked once more at Joan and then obeyed her. The next morning he gave Joan a suit of **armour** and a helmet and a sword. She cut her beautiful hair short so that her helmet could fit over it. She took the sword and rode off on a fine horse which the captain had given her.

At last she got to the court of King Charles, who finally agreed to give her a small army to go to the city of Orleans which was being attacked by the English.

Joan entering Orleans

The English had built towers all around the city of Orleans and from the top of these towers they were shooting arrows over the walls of the city. They hoped to force the people of Orleans to give up the city and open the gates so that they could capture it.

You can imagine how surprised they were when they saw an army approaching, headed by a girl. They were too surprised even to shoot and Joan marched between the towers and entered the city.

When she was safely inside with her army, Joan called together all the citizens of Orleans.

'Do not be afraid,' she told them. 'I have been sent by God to drive the enemy away from France. Tomorrow we shall drive the English away from Orleans.'

Joan fighting against the English

The next morning the city gates opened and Joan came riding out at the head of her army. A shower of arrows greeted them and Joan was shot in the arm. Blood flowed down over the **banner** which she carried. When the French soldiers saw this, they were encouraged. They looked at Joan; even though she had been wounded, she was fighting the English with all their strength. The English were driven back and the city of Orleans was saved.

Joan won many battles, but at last she was captured by the English and thrown into prison. The English wanted her to admit that she was a **witch** and a liar but Joan refused. Every day they questioned her. They did not let her sleep at nights, but went on hour after hour with their questions. Joan refused to give in. Even though she became thin and weak in prison and realized that she would soon die, she was not afraid.

Did you know?

Joan was known as La Pucelle, which means 'the maid'. Joan is often known as the Maid of Orleans. because she saved the city of Orleans.

At last the court, which could not make her confess, condemned her to die. Joan was taken to the centre of the town and placed on a great pile of dry wood. Her hands were tied behind her and she was bound with strong ropes to a huge stake of wood.

Joan at the stake

'Burn her!' cried the people. 'Let her die, she is a witch!' They did not know the truth because the English had made them believe that Joan was a liar. Someone stepped forward and set fire to the wood. The flames roared and crackled and slowly crept up towards Joan. Soon they reached her feet and then her dress caught fire.

'A cross! a cross! If only I had a cross to hold at this moment!' cried Joan.

One of the English soldiers reached down and quickly made a rough cross out of two pieces of wood. He handed it up to Joan and she reached out an arm through the smoke and clasped it to her heart. Then the flames covered her. Most of the people were happy, but the soldier who gave her the cross said to his friends, 'They say she was a devil, but I think she was an angel. We have burnt a saint.'

Many years later, in 1920, the Catholic Church declared that Joan of Arc was indeed a **saint**, and today she is known as Saint Joan.

Exercises

1. **Answer the following.**
   (a) What did the angel tell Joan?
   (b) Why did both the sentry and the captain obey Joan's demand?

(c) How did the English punish Joan?

(d) Why did the English soldier give Joan a cross?

(e) Why is Joan of Arc known as Saint Joan?

2. Fill in the blanks.

(a) Joan of Arc lived more than .... hundred years ago.

(b) She was born in .... and her parents were simple ....

(c) In the woods near her home Joan heard the voice of an ....

(d) Joan went to see the .... who was the most important officer in her district.

(e) The English were attacking the city of ....

3. Give one word answers.

(a) Name the ruler of France when Joan was seventeen years old.

(b) Name the country that was at war with France.

(c) What did Joan want to hold when she was being burnt?

(d) Who declared Joan of Arc as a saint?

Things to do

1. For your scrapbook!

What kind of helmet do you think Joan wore in the battle? Try to find pictures of armour, swords and shields used at the time that Joan lived and stick them in your book.

2. Find out!

India has also had many brave women who had the courage to fight their enemies. One such woman was the Rani of Jhansi. Try and find an interesting fact about her and share it with the class.

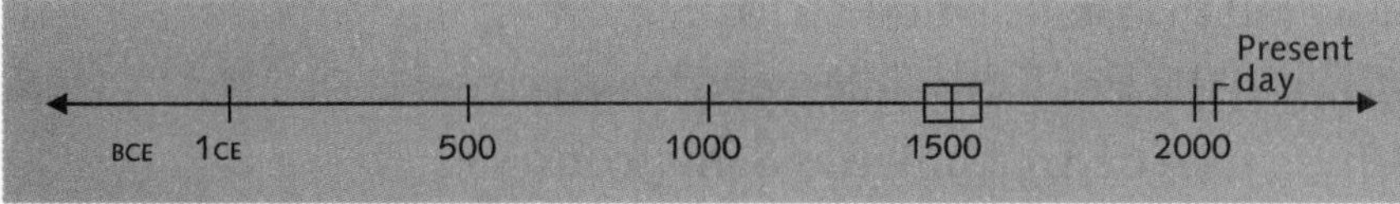

6

Kabir

—The great mystic-poet

Kabir Das was a poet and **mystic** who was born around 600 years ago at Benaras. It is said that he was an abandoned child who was brought up by a Muslim weaver named Niru and his wife Nima.

As Kabir grew up, he was influenced by a Hindu **ascetic**, Ramananda. He was determined to become Ramananda's disciple. In those days it was difficult to even imagine that a Brahmin would have accepted a poor weaver as his disciple.

One day Kabir went to the bank of the river Ganges in Benaras and waited for Ramananda to come back after taking his bath in the river. When Swami Ramananda came back, Kabir immediately caught hold of his feet. Such an act would normally have outraged a Brahmin, especially after a bath.

But Ramananda was a saint. He asked, 'My son, what do you want?' Kabir replied, 'Sir, make me your disciple.'
And Swami Ramananda immediately agreed. Ramananda's followers objected saying, 'Sir, he is an orphan, brought up in a Muslim

Words to remember

mystic : a person who becomes united with God through prayers and meditation.

ascetic : one who does not allow oneself physical pleasures, especially for religious reasons.

reverence : a feeling of great respect and admiration for something or somebody.

family. How can you do that? He will not accept any of the principles from the Hindu religion.'

Ramananda looked at Kabir and he could see a great seeker there. He could immediately understand that they were both seekers of truth. He replied, 'You don't know him. I know him.'

Kabir

And he took Kabir with him and Kabir became a great saint under Ramananda.

Kabir respected his guru Ramananda, but there were differences in their understanding of reality. While Kabir was against many age-old rituals of Hinduism, Ramananda still held some of them in **reverence**. But despite these differences, Ramananda allowed Kabir to grow in his own way. In due course, it was the guru who changed.

Kabir tried to unite the Hindus and Muslims. He preached the unity of all religions and the equality of all men. Kabir rejected the outward show of religions and believed in inward worship and remembrance of God. He said, 'God is to be found, not in the temple, but inside our own heart.'

Instead of choosing the Hindu religion or Islam, Kabir took the best teachings of both the religions. From Hinduism, he accepted the idea of *karma*. This means our lives are governed by our actions. From Islam, he accepted the idea of one God and the equality of human beings before God. The ideas of the Muslim mystics, called Sufis, also influenced him greatly. He called his set of preachings, *sahaja-yoga*, which means 'simple union'.

Kabir strongly recommended non-violence and vegetarianism. Kabir always believed in the idea of *Koi bole Ram Ram, Koi Khudai...*, which means that someone may chant the Hindu name of God and someone may chant the Muslim name of God, but God is the one who made the whole world. Kabir's followers are known as Kabirpanthis. They worship one God and preach in the local or regional language. The guru or the religious teacher is central to the faith and greatly respected.

Kabir in discussion with a disciple

Like the teachings of his guru Ramananda, who was a Bhakti saint, Kabir's teachings too contributed to the Bhakti Movement. Some of Kabir's ideas were used in Sikhism as well. Sikhism was started a little after the time of Kabir, by Nanak. Some of Kabir's poetry was included in the *Adi Granth*, the holy book of the Sikhs.

There are many incidents and stories about Kabir's life which illustrate his beliefs. It is said that once, when a Sultan was visiting Benares, the King of Benares was persuaded to call Kabir. When Kabir arrived in the court, he merely offered a common greeting. The Sultan's minister asked, 'Why don't you bow and humble yourself before the Sultan?'

Kabir replied, 'There is only one king in this world—God—and the same god lives in all people—Hindus and Muslims.'

Did you know?

A book called *Bijak* was composed by one of Kabir's disciples. It contains Kabir's *dohas* and teachings.

The Sultan was impressed by Kabir's answer and said, 'You are a true lover of God'.

Kabir wrote many poems and songs, and expressed his teachings in the form of two-line poems or *dohas*. It is believed that Kabir wrote approximately two thousand songs and fifteen hundred couplets. These songs and couplets are popular even today. His songs and sayings were for everyone. These were written in Hindi, and his teachings were expressed in simple language. His poetry contributed to the development of Hindi literature. Many of his songs were later translated into English by the poet, Rabindranath Tagore.

Kabir died in Maghar in 1518 CE. When he died, it is said, Maghar's usually dry stream was restored to a year-round river of water. On his death a dispute arose over his body. The Hindu and Muslim disciples both wanted his remains. The Muslims wanted to bury the body while the Hindus wanted to cremate it. When the cloth was removed, there was no body to be seen—only flowers. His tomb and *samadhi* still stand side by side.

Exercises

1. **Answer the following.**
   (a) How did Kabir become Ramananda's disciple?
   (b) Describe any two teachings of Kabir.
   (c) Who are Kabirpanthis?
   (d) What principles did Kabir accept from Islam?

2. **Fill in the blanks.**
   (a) Kabir was born around .... at ....
   (b) A book called .... , composed of Kabir's verses and observations, was completed by a disciple.
   (c) Many of Kabir's songs were later translated into English by the poet, ...
   (d) Kabir called his set of preachings ....

3. **Match the following.**

(a) Sufis	Simple union
(b) Ramananda	Benaras
(c) A holy city	Muslim mystics
(d) Sahaja-yoga	Kabir's guru

Things to do

1. **For your scrapbook!**
   Collect pictures of Kabir, Guru Nanak, Mirabai or any other great saint. Paste them in your book.
2. **Find out!**
   Complete the following *dohas* written by Kabir and recite them in your class. Discuss their meaning with your teachers and classmates.
   (a) *Dukh mein sumiran sab* ....
   (b) *Kaal kare so aaj kar* ....

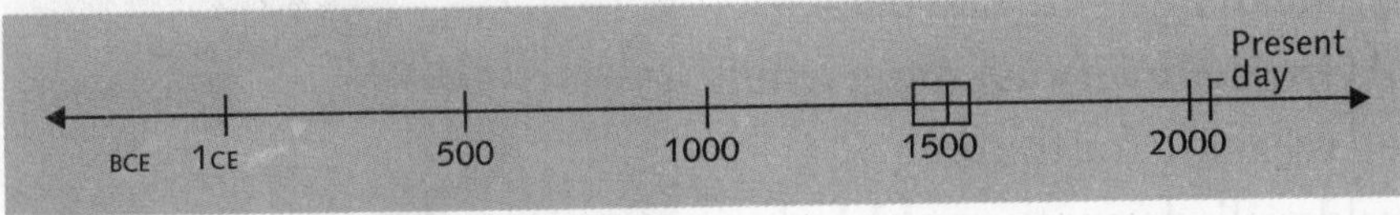

Christopher Columbus

—The man who discovered America

7

In the fifteenth century, Europeans knew very little about Africa and Asia. They had read about Asia in books. They thought that these were wonderful places with strange birds, rivers of gold, rich kings with jewels and precious stones and many other things. Marco Polo had brought back wonderful stories of the East. It was not until 200 years after Marco Polo that seamen from Europe began their **explorations**. The first voyages of exploration were led by two European countries—Spain and Portugal. One of the most famous of these explorers was Christopher Columbus.

Christopher Columbus was born in Genoa in 1451 CE. Genoa is on the west coast of Italy. Christopher's father was a weaver. When he was a small boy Christopher helped his father in his work. He did not like the work much and spent most of his time at the harbour with his best friend, Lorenzo, who was an old sailor. Lorenzo was Christopher's hero. He had sailed all

Words to remember

exploration : the act of travelling through a place in order to find out about it.

cobbled : paved with smooth round stones.

pirates : sea robbers.

discovery : an act or process of finding or learning about something that was not known before.

threaten : express an intention to punish or hurt.

aground : (of ships) touching the bottom in shallow water.

inhabitants : persons living in a place.

over the Mediterranean Sea—he had been to Spain, Africa and Greece. Every evening, when his father finished weaving for the day, Christopher would walk down the **cobbled** streets of Genoa to meet Lorenzo, who would tell him wonderful stories about Spanish ships, about the deserts and cities of Africa. He told him how he had been captured by **pirates** near the coast of Greece and how he had escaped. He told him about great storms at sea, when the wind whistled in the sails and the waves swept over the deck.

Christopher Columbus

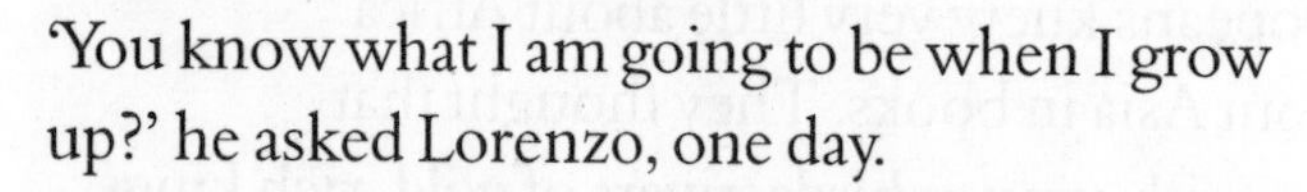

'You know what I am going to be when I grow up?' he asked Lorenzo, one day.

'Yes,' said Lorenzeo. 'You are going to be a weaver like your father.'

'No, I am not,' said Christopher. 'I am going to be a sailor.'

'It is not easy to become a sailor these days,' said Lorenzo.

'What do you mean?' asked Christopher.

'The Arabs have taken all our trade,' said Lorenzo. 'We used to take ships down to Egypt and then go down through the Indian Ocean. But the Arabs have stopped all that; we can't get to Asia any more.'

Before Christopher Columbus was born, most people thought that the world was flat. But about this time people began to think that the earth was round, like an orange. Christopher talked to Lorenzo about it.

'If the land called India is in the east,' he said, 'and if the world is like an orange, why can't we go round the other way? If we go west, we shall surely get to India.'

Christopher grew up and he thought more and more about this idea. He became a sailor and made many voyages across the Mediterranean. He had fights with pirates; he went past Gibraltar and visited France and England.

In 1477 CE, Columbus went to live in Portugal, and married the daughter of a sea captain. This sea captain had made many voyages and had explored the western coast of Africa. Columbus decided that he would like to make a voyage of **discovery** too. He still thought that if he went west he would find India.

At last Columbus took his plans to the king of Portugal. The king was certainly interested in finding another route to India, but the king's advisers told him that it was an impossible plan and that it would never succeed.

Columbus presenting his idea

Columbus then went to Spain and asked the king and the queen of Spain to help him. They, too, were interested in his plans. They were the rivals of Portugal and would have liked to get to India first. Unfortunately Spain was at war and ten years passed before the Queen of Spain agreed to send Columbus on his voyage. She gave him three ships, but Columbus found it very difficult to get seamen. When he did get the seamen, they refused to sail with him when he told them that they were going on a voyage to the unknown.

At last in 1492 CE, when Columbus had managed to find nearly ninety men, he set out on his famous voyage. He first went towards the Canary Island in the Atlantic Ocean. From there the winds blew to the west and Columbus knew that he could sail his ships in the direction he wanted. His chief worry was the crew. Neither he nor they knew exactly where they were going. No one knew how long the voyage would take. Columbus was afraid that if the men knew how far away they were from Spain they would protest and refuse to work. He knew that if they did so he would have to return. So he thought of a plan. Every captain on a voyage was to keep a logbook to note down the distance covered, etc.

The king and queen of Spain seeing off Columbus

Columbus kept two logbooks. In one, he put the real distances which the ship had travelled; in the second, he put false statements to show that they had not travelled as far as they had. He showed this second logbook to his officers and men. In this way, the crew never knew how far away they were from Spain.

They sailed on and on, week after week. Everything went well. There were no storms, the sea was calm and they had plenty of food. But soon the men began to worry. One morning, after they had been at sea for thirty days, one of the officers came to Columbus in his cabin.

'What do you want?' asked Columbus.

'We have sailed far enough,' said the officer. 'There is no land in sight. We have been at sea for thirty days.'

Columbus pretended to look carefully at his charts. 'There is no need to worry,' he said. 'We shall reach land in a day or two.'

'How can you be sure?' asked the officer.

'I'm a good sailor, that is why!' said Columbus. 'Two days is not too long to wait, is it?'

'Well,' said the officer. 'You have been telling us to wait for a long time. The crew and officers are frightened. Every time I meet them they **threaten** me.'

'All right,' said Columbus. 'If we don't reach land within two days, I shall agree to return. Tell the crew that,' Luckily Columbus was right. Just two days later, at two o'clock in the morning, one of the men sitting on the deck shouted, 'Land, Land!'

Columbus came running out of his cabin and in the moonlight he could see the waves breaking on the shore a few miles away. Columbus had reached the Caribbean Islands. They anchored the boats offshore, and as soon as the sun was up they landed on the islands. The people of the islands wore tiny gold rings in their noses. Columbus had seen pictures of Indians wearing similar gold ornaments.

'I'm right!' he cried. 'We have reached the Indies and these people are Indians. We shall go round India and after that we shall get to Japan.'

He set sail again and after two weeks he discovered Cuba. He immediately sent off a little band of people to go and visit the Japanese Emperor. They were disappointed! Then Columbus went back to his charts. He worked all night. In the morning he told his men, 'This is not Japan! I have made a serious mistake; it is China.'

A replica of the Santa Maria

For the next three months Columbus sailed round the island. Unfortunately one dark night, one of his ships, the *Santa Maria,* went **aground** and was wrecked. Columbus used wood from this ship to build a small fort. He left forty men in the fort and returned home to get more ships.

While he was sailing home, Columbus wrote a long letter to the king and queen of Spain. He told them of the islands he had visited near the Chinese coast. He told them that the islands grew wonderful spices. He told them about the beautiful mountains and the beautiful birds. He also told them how much gold there was in the island. Had he not seen the gold ornaments in the noses of the **inhabitants**?

When he arrived in Spain, the king and queen entertained him at their palace. They made him an admiral and listened to all his stories of the islands near China. They agreed to send him back on another voyage and hoped that he would bring back great quantities of gold, which would make Spain the richest country in Europe.

In 1493 CE, Columbus set sail and again he found the islands with their palm trees and white beaches. But he could see no sign of the Chinese. He went back to the little fort he had built. Each of the forty men had been killed by the

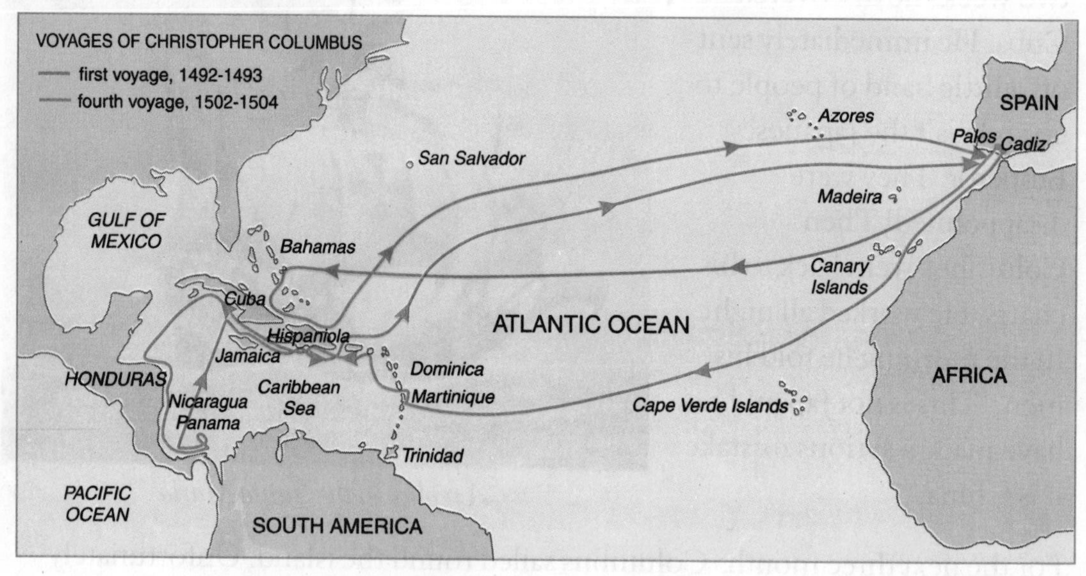

Discoveries of Columbus

islanders. He sailed on still farther. He thought he had come to Malaya, but instead he discovered Jamaica.

At last he stopped. His ships needed repairs and his crew was tired, so he sailed back to Spain. He made another voyage and then another. Every time he came back to Spain he brought promises of gold. Sometimes he brought home slaves from the islands, and when they got to Spain they were sent to work in the mines. But he never found gold and he never found India. He did not realize that he had discovered America. He was still greatly honoured in Spain, however. He died in 1506 CE. He was the first man to cross the Atlantic Ocean. It was his early voyages that made it possible for other explorers to discover other parts of America.

Did you know?

Horses were first introduced in the Americas by Christopher Columbus during his second voyage and tobacco was introduced into Europe after Columbus had seen it being used by the Native Americans.

Exercises

1. **Answer the following.**
   (a) Why did Columbus want to become a sailor?
   (b) Why did Columbus think of finding a different route to India?
   (c) Why did the king of Portugal refuse to help Columbus?
   (d) Why did Columbus take the Caribbean Islands as India?
   (e) Who financed Columbus's voyage and why?
   (f) Why did Columbus keep two logbooks?

2. **Say whether the following are True or False.**
   (a) Columbus was born in Venice.
   (b) Columbus set out on his famous voyage in 1492.
   (c) The ship which went aground was called the *Santa Maria*.
   (d) Columbus was the first man to sail across the Pacific Ocean.
   (e) Columbus finally succeeded in discovering India.

3. **Match the following.**

(a) Columbus discovered	Was a sailor
(b) Columbus's father	Was a weaver
(c) Lorenzo	Was financed by the queen of Spain
(d) Columbus's voyage	America

Things to do

1. **For your scrapbook.**
   Draw a picture of an old sailing ship or collect pictures of different types of ships and boats. Stick them in your book.

2. **Map work.**
   On an outline map of the world mark the following oceans: Atlantic Ocean; Pacific Ocean; Indian Ocean; Arctic Ocean.

3. **Check the following websites for some interesting information.**
   http://www.enchantedlearning.com/explorers/page/c/columbus.shtml (accessed on 14 August 2006)
   http://bbc.co.uk/history/historic_figures/christopher_columbus.shtml (accessed on 14 August 2006)

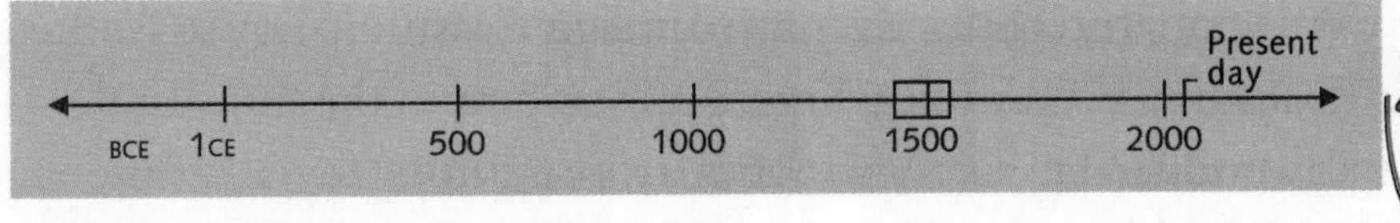

Leonardo da Vinci

—A universal genius

Leonardo da Vinci was a great master of both arts and science. He was a painter, sculptor, architect, musician, engineer, inventor and scientist. He is considered as one of the greatest painters that ever lived.

Leonardo da Vinci was born in 1452 CE in a small town near Florence named Vinci. He was the son of a wealthy **notary** and a peasant woman.

In the mid-1460s, their family settled in Florence, where Leonardo was given the best education. He was a great artist even as a child.

Leonardo da Vinci

Words to remember

notary : a person with official authority to be a witness when somebody signs a document.
apprentice : a person who works for an employer to learn the skill.
guild : an association of craftsmen or merchants.
patron : a person who gives money and support to artists or writers.
mural : a painting done on a wall.
portraits : a painting, drawing or photograph of a person.
celebrated : famous.
legendary : very famous and talked about a lot.

In his teenage years, Leonardo became an **apprentice** as a studio boy to Andrea del Verrocchio, the leading Florentine painter and sculptor of the time. In the workshop, he was introduced to many activities, from painting to the creation of large sculptures in marble and bronze. In 1472 CE, he joined the painter's **guild** of Florence.

At first, it was difficult for Leonardo to get **patrons**. To impress Ludovico Sforza, the duke of Milan, he wrote a long letter describing his talents. He listed nine different wartime projects like portable bridges, ships, armoured vehicles, catapults and cannons that he would take on if given the chance. Leonardo wrote:

'I believe I am capable of giving you as much satisfaction as anyone, whether it be in architecture, for the construction of public or private buildings, or in bringing water from one place to another... I can sculpt in marble, bronze, or terracotta; while in painting, my work is the equal of anyone's.'

Madonna of the Rocks

The letter was eventually accepted and in 1482 CE, Leonardo entered the service of Sforza. He served there as a principal military engineer and also as an architect.

During the early Milan days, the most important paintings he created were the *Madonna of the Rocks* and *The Virgin of the Rocks*. It was his usual practice to work on the paintings for a long time, as if he was unwilling to finish what he had begun.

From 1495 to 1497 CE, Leonardo worked hard on his masterpiece, *The Last Supper*, a huge 15 x 29 feet **mural** in the monastery of Santa Maria delle Grazie, Milan. It is a scene showing Christ with his disciples in the evening, a few

The Last Supper

seconds after Christ revealed to them that one disciple would betray him before sunrise. While all the twelve disciples have reacted to the news with different degrees of horror, anger and shock, Christ is shown calm in the midst of the storm.

The Duke permitted Leonardo to operate his own workshop, complete with apprentices. He was provided seventy tons of bronze for making *Gran Cavallo*, a huge statue of a horse. Unfortunately, the bronze had to be cast into weapons for the Duke to save Milan from the French attack in 1495 CE.

The Gran Cavallo

When the French returned in 1498 CE, Milan fell without a fight, overthrowing Duke Sforza. Leonardo stayed in Milan for a time, until one morning when he found French archers using his life-size clay model of the horse for target practice. He left Milan immediately with some of his friends.

Leonardo returned to Florence and in 1502 CE, he entered the service of Cesare Borgia, Duke of Romagna. As the duke's chief architect and engineer, Leonardo supervised work on the fortresses in central Italy.

During this time in Florence, Leonardo painted several **portraits**, but the only one that survives is the famous *Mona Lisa*. *Mona Lisa*, painted during 1503–06 CE, is one of the most **celebrated** portraits ever painted. *Mona Lisa* is well known for the mystery of its **legendary** smile. Leonardo had a special affection for the picture and he took it with him during his travels. Although Leonardo produced a small number of paintings, many of which remained unfinished, he was nevertheless an extraordinarily talented artist.

Mona Lisa

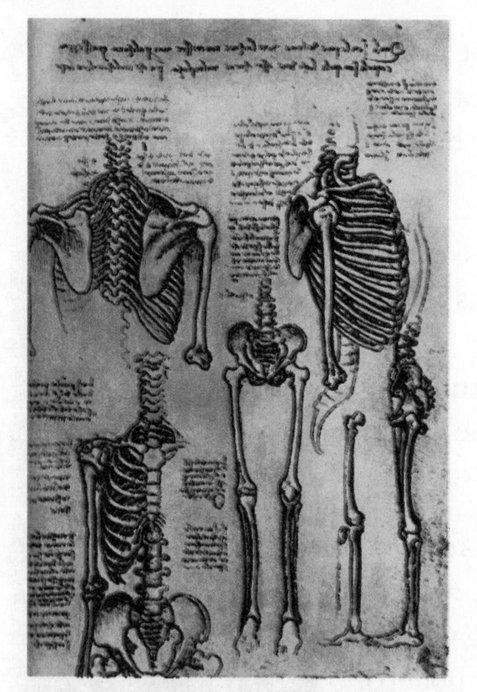

Leonardo's drawings of the human body were very detailed

A notable characteristic of Leonardo's paintings is landscape backgrounds.

Many a time, Leonardo was asked by the government to design state buildings or churches, or to make up new weapons. He designed many inventions, such as the helicopter, tank, use of solar power, and the calculator, that became a reality in the future with the help of modern technology. He invented a large number of useful machines, among them an underwater diving suit.

Leonardo wanted to understand and know about everything he saw. He examined all of nature; how plants and trees grow, how rocks are formed and how the wind flows. Leonardo's scientific theories were based on careful observation. There are a lot of scientific experiments that were recorded in his sketches. Leonardo, before his death, made many drawings of the human body. There are detailed drawings of skeletons, muscle structures, and organ systems.

Leonardo had ideas about many things long before they were thought of in modern times. He also made discoveries in medicine, meteorology and geography.

Leonardo spent his last years at the Château de Cloux, where he died in 1519 CE. He was a great genius who had a deep love of knowledge and research, which he used in both his artistic and scientific works. His fresh ideas in the field of painting influenced the course of Italian art for more than a century after his death.

Did you know?

Leonardo's scientific theories are contained in numerous notebooks, most of which were written in mirror-image script from right to left i.e. his writing had to be read in a mirror.

Exercises

1. **Answer the following.**
   (a) How did Leonardo da Vinci impress Ludovico Sforza?
   (b) Describe the masterpiece, 'The Last Supper' by Leonardo.
   (c) Why did Leonardo leave Milan in the 1498 CE?
   (d) How would you describe the creative genius of Leonardo.

2. Fill in the blanks.

(a) Leonardo was the son of a wealthy .... and a .... woman.

(b) A notable characteristic of Leonardo's paintings is .... backgrounds.

(c) *The Last Supper* is a huge ....

(d) Leonardo spent his last years at the ...., where he died in 1519.

3. Match the following.

(a) Mona Lisa	Duke of Milan
(b) Andrea del Verrocchio	A huge statue of a horse
(c) Ludovico Sforza	Painter and sculptor
(d) Gran Cavallo	Duke of Romagna
(e) Cesare Borgia	Legendary smile

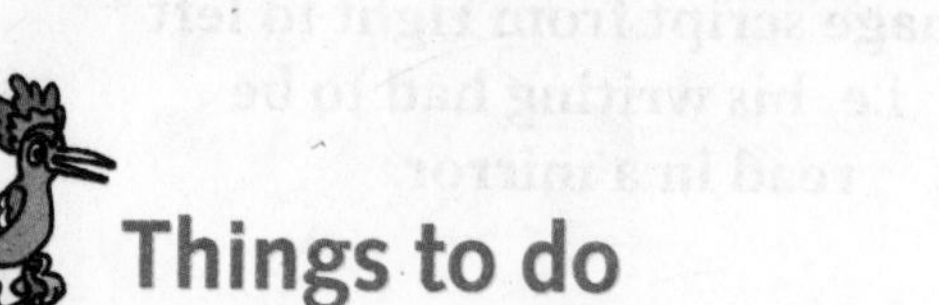

Things to do

1. For your scrapbook!

Collect the photos of paintings and drawings by Leonardo da Vinci and paste them in a scrapbook. You may like to include his famous paintings like *Mona Lisa, The Last Supper, Madonna and Child*; and his drawings of helicopter, tank, human body, calculator etc.

2. Make leaf designs.

Make a picture composition with various leaf shapes. One has been done for you.

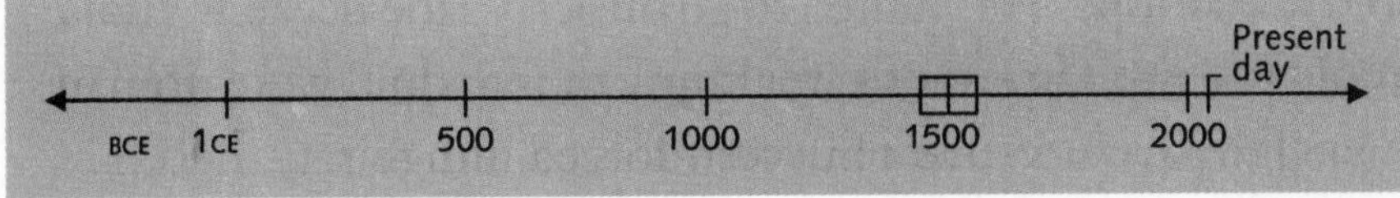

9

Vasco da Gama
—The first European to reach India

Spain took the Europeans to the American continent. Portugal showed Europe the sea route to Asia. Portugal, on the west coast of Spain, had many brave sailors. The Portuguese had good ships and their seamen were used to sailing in the rough waters of the Atlantic. These seamen took their ships farther and farther down the coast of Africa. The men who made these voyages were brave. They never knew what they would find or what **adventures** they would have. The government of Portugal wanted to keep all these journeys secret. They wanted to trade with Africa and they did not want other people in Europe to find out about it.

The Portuguese were anxious to go past Africa to the countries beyond it. They wanted spices, such as cinnamon and cloves, and they also wanted slaves. Some of their explorers reached the southernmost part of Africa.

In 1487 CE, the king of Portugal sent Bartholomew Diaz on a voyage to find the southernmost point of Africa. He reached the south of Africa and sailed

Words to remember

adventure : excitement associated with danger, taking risks, etc.
cabin : room in a ship.
palanquin : a covered couch for one person, carried on poles by two or more people, as used in India.
kidnapped : taken away by force and illegally, especially in order to obtain money in return for releasing the prisoners.

round the Cape of Good Hope. He wanted to go on across the ocean to India but his men refused. They had been at sea for many months and were tired of the voyage. Diaz tried to persuade them but they forced him to return to Portugal.

A few years later, however, the king of Portugal decided to send a man called Vasco da Gama on another voyage. Vasco da Gama was thirty-seven years old at the time. He decided to take four ships with him. Diaz came to the harbour to give his advice about the ships. Men worked day and night to get them ready. On the day before he was to sail, Vasco da Gama had dinner with Diaz in his **cabin**. They sat late over their food.

'It will be a long and dangerous journey,' said Diaz, 'but do not follow my route along the coast.'

'Why not?' asked Vasco da Gama.

'Because you will fail!' said Diaz.

'There are terrible storms near the coast. I advise you to keep away from the coast and go far out into the Atlantic. When you have gone as far as possible, that will be the time to turn towards Africa.'

Vasco da Gama

'I shall take your advice,' said Vasco da Gama. 'I shall reach India or die in the attempt.'

Next day, on 8 July 1497, Vasco da Gama left Lisbon. He sailed down to the Verde Islands and met with a terrible storm there. After that they kept well away from the coast and went down south, through the Atlantic Ocean. For three months, they saw no land at all. Finally, Vasco da Gama turned towards Africa and reached Saint Helena Bay. They landed there, and took fresh food and water. But they were soon off again and passed round the southernmost part of Africa. They sailed on and on, hundreds of miles, until they came to the coast of Mozambique.

Vasco da Gama continued up the coast with many adventures. At last he got to Mombasa. The people of Mombasa did not like the Portuguese. They were afraid of them and thought they had come to harm them. However, Vasco da Gama captured two men and questioned them. He wanted to find out whether it was safe to continue his voyage. When they did not answer him properly, he poured boiling oil on their arms to get them to speak the truth.

Vasco da Gama in Mombasa

He next sailed from Mombasa to Malindi, a little way along the coast, and there he found some Hindus living. He also found a Gujarati pilot, who agreed to show him the way across the Indian Ocean.

After many days at sea, on 20 May 1498 CE, Vasco da Gama arrived at Calicut, which is now known as Kozhikode. Kozhikode in those days was under the rule of a king called Zamorin. It was a rich and prosperous town and there were many Arab traders. You can imagine how surprised the people were to see men from Europe. Vasco da Gama was taken in a **palanquin** carried by four people to see Zamorin. In front of him walked a priest and behind the priest there were men from the ship carrying candles and crosses.

Vasco da Gama arriving at Calicut

'We can give you spices, pepper and precious stones,' said Zamorin. 'But what have you got for us? Strings of beads and cheap cloth! What we want from you is gold and silver. Go back to your country; if you bring us gold we shall certainly give you spices.'

Vasco da Gama left the palace of Zamorin feeling sad that he could not take back spices and precious stones to Portugal.

'I shall go home and bring back gold and silver,' he said to himself. 'I shall fight these Arab traders, too, and get their business.'

But suddenly, out of the dark, a crowd of men appeared. They thrust a bag over Vasco da Gama's head and before he knew what was happening, his arms were tied to his sides and he was taken away. On the ship, da Gama's brother waited for him until late that night. At last, when Vasco da Gama did not return, his brother sent two or three men to find out whether he was still at Zamorin's palace. The men did not return until next morning, and when they did, they told da Gama's brother that Vasco had been **kidnapped**. Within an hour Vasco's brother had captured six of the most important men in Calicut. Then he called a meeting in the marketplace.

Did you know?

Vasco da Gama took with him on his voyage a number of big stone pillars called *padroes*. As he went along, he set these up on the land to mark the discoveries that he had made.

'You have taken my brother,' he said to the people, 'but I have taken six of your brothers. Unless Vasco is returned before sunset we shall sail away to Portugal, and you will never see your brothers again.'

Vasco da Gama was soon released and they set sail for Portugal. They left Calicut in August, but it took them six months to reach Malindi on the African coast. They had bad winds and storms and many of the crew were sick. They had to leave one ship at Mozambique because they did not have enough sailors.

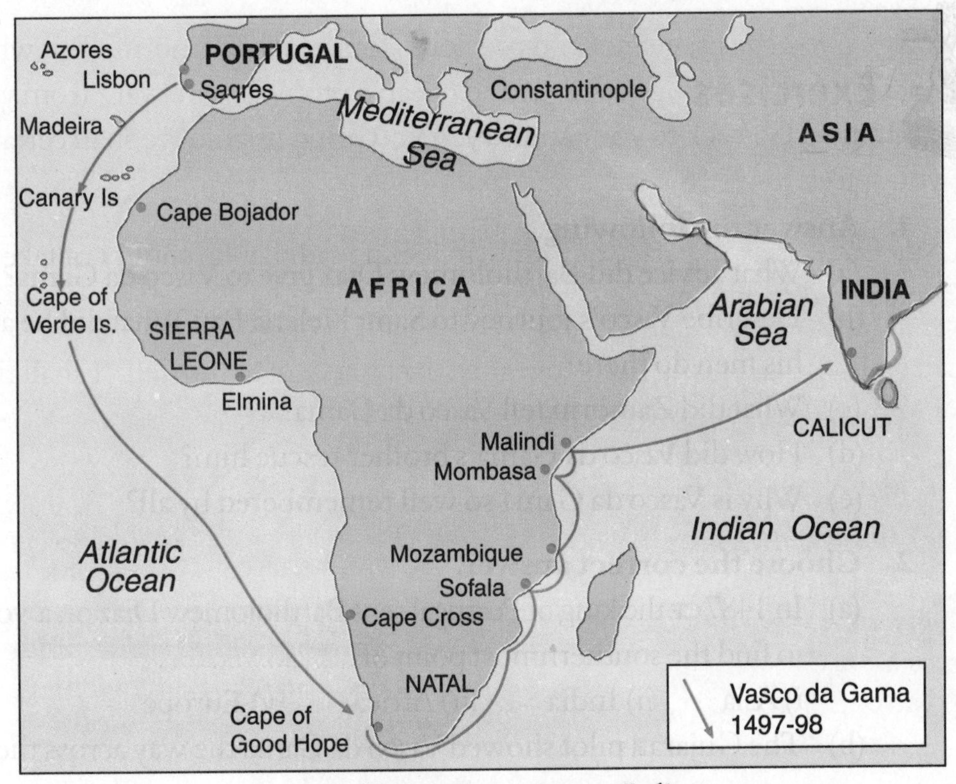

Vasco da Gama's sea route to India

They struggled round the coast of Africa and got back to Lisbon in September, more than a year after they had left Calicut. Two years earlier, Vasco da Gama had left Lisbon with 170 men; he returned with less than 50.

In 1502 CE, Vasco da Gama sailed once more to India. This time he took ten ships with him. He attacked Calicut fiercely and sank many of the Arab ships which took spices from Calicut to Africa. People on the coast were afraid of him, but they also helped him. They were glad when he sailed back to Portugal with his ships full of jewels and spices. When he got back to Portugal he became very rich. After twenty years, he sailed once more to India. He had been sent by the king of Portugal to rule over the Portuguese colonies on the west coast of India. He died at Cochin (now Kochi) in 1524 CE.

Exercises

1. **Answer the following.**
   (a) What advice did Bartholomew Diaz give to Vasco da Gama?
   (b) Describe Vasco's journey to Saint Helena Bay. What did he and his men do there?
   (c) What did Zamorin tell Vasco da Gama?
   (d) How did Vasco da Gama's brother rescue him?
   (e) Why is Vasco da Gama so well remembered by all?

2. **Choose the correct answer.**
   (a) In 1487 CE the king of Portugal sent Bartholomew Diaz on a voyage to find the southernmost point of ....
   i) Asia ii) India iii) Africa iv) Europe
   (b) The Gujarati pilot showed Vasco da Gama the way across the ....
   i) Atlantic Ocean ii) Pacific Ocean iii) Indian Ocean iv) Arctic Ocean
   (c) Vasco da Gama arrived at Calicut in .... CE.
   i) 1477 ii) 1498 iii) 1484 iv) 1559
   (d) Vasco da Gama died at .... in 1524 CE.
   i) Cochin ii) Kozhikode iii) Mombasa iv) Lisbon

3. **Say whether the following are True or False.**
   (a) The Portuguese were anxious to explore the countries beyond Africa.
   (b) Vasco da Gama sailed down to the Verde Islands and met with a terrible storm there.
   (c) Vasco da Gama went on foot to see Zamorin.
   (d) Zamorin was the ruler of India during the time of Vasco's visit.
   (e) Vasco da Gama was the first European to reach India by sea.

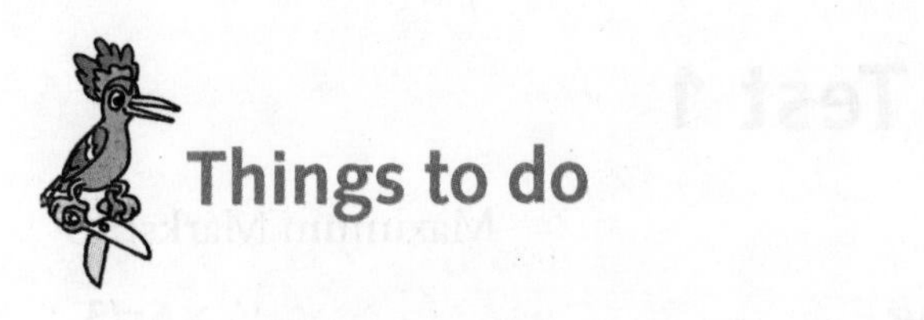

Things to do

1. **Map work.**
   On an outline map of the world, mark Vasco da Gama's sea route to India.

2. **Find out!**
   The ship below contains jumbled words connected with this chapter. Unscramble the jumbled words and write them down in the blank spaces given.

CHINOC
GEVAOY
RINMOZA
ZIAD
GORPUTAL
BILSNO
BASAMMO
TANALCIT

Unit Test 1

Maximum Marks: 15

1. Give one word for the following. ½ ×6=3

(a) The holy writings of a religion
(b) A person who becomes united with god through prayers and meditation
(c) The book containing Kabir's *dohas*
(d) A protective covering usually made of metal worn when fighting
(e) A painting done on a wall
(f) The writings of the four disciples of Christ

2. Answer the following. 2×4=8

(a) Name the holy book of the Christians. What does it contain?
(b) Mention the five rules that guide all Muslims.
(c) Why is the Nalanda University famous?
(d) What were the teachings of Kabir?

3. Fill in the blanks. ½×4=2

(a) Nicolo and Maffeo Polo visited the great king.......
(b) Christopher Columbus discovered......
(c) Leonardo da Vinci is famous for his painting known as............
(d) The famous Chinese traveller.........visited India during the reign of Harsha.

4. On an outline map of the world mark the following. ½×4=2

(a) Bethlehem
(b) Mecca
(c) Italy
(d) France

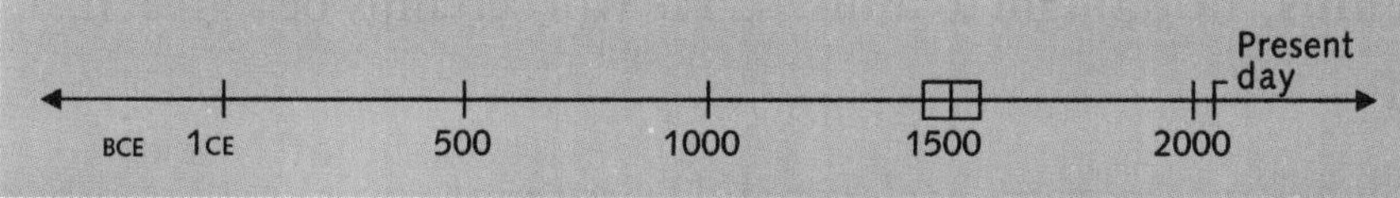

10

Guru Nanak
—The founder of the Sikh religion

Guru Nanak was born more than 500 years ago. He was the first of the ten Sikh Gurus and the founder of the Sikh religion. He was born in North India, and even when he was young he was quite different from other children. He learned to walk and talk at a very early age and people said they had never seen such a child. He was so clever that when he was taken to school he began to question his teacher.

An old painting showing Guru Nanak being taken to school

'What is the use of all this learning Panditji?' he asked. 'The only true learning comes from God. Can you tell me why some people are rich and some people poor?'

The teacher was quite unable to answer this question.

After a year Guru Nanak was taken away from the village school and sent to the mosque. The maulvi of the mosque began to teach him Persian. He learnt so quickly that the **maulvi** was amazed.

Words to remember

maulvi : Muslim priest.
genius : person having great creative capacity.
gypsies : members of a wandering Asiatic race.
wretched : of poor quality.
ancestors : forefathers.

'This child is a **genius**,' he thought to himself. 'He will certainly be a great man when he grows up.'

Although Guru Nanak was extremely clever and learnt more quickly than other boys, he was also a great dreamer. He spent many hours in the woods and fields. He loved to smell the grass, to listen to the birds and to watch them making their nests. On many occasions, when his father and mother sent him out to look after the cows, Nanak would take the cows to some grassy place and let them graze. Then he would sit down and dream, not realizing that the cows had wandered away or had eaten crops growing in the neighbouring field.

Sometimes his father and mother would give him money to buy things. Nanak would come back empty-handed.

'Where are the things you bought, Nanak?'

'What things?'

'Did we not give you money this morning to buy cloth?'

'Yes, mother.'

'Where is the money?'

'I have no money.'

'Then where is the cloth?'

'I have no cloth either. I met some poor **gypsies** on the river bank. I gave them the money to buy food.'

'So what about our cloth?'

'You are rich, mother, but they were hungry. Did I do wrong by helping them?'

His father and mother could say nothing to him. However, they thought that Nanak would become responsible if he got married. So, at the age of sixteen,

Nanak was married. As the years went by, Nanak had two sons. But even then, he spent very little time with his family. He hardly took notice of his wife and sons; he spent most of his time in thinking about God and in saying his prayers.

When Nanak continued like this, his sister, Nanaki, became worried.

'If Nanak goes on like this,' she told her husband Jai Ram, 'his wife and his children will starve. He never thinks of food or the house or clothing for his family.'

'Why don't we bring him to Sultanpur? I am sure Khan Sahib will give him some work,' said her husband.

'That's a good idea,' said his wife. 'If he has some regular work, perhaps he will look after his family better.'

So Nanak went to Sultanpur where the Khan Sahib gave him a job as a storekeeper. He had to look after the stores, to pay for the new stores and to keep the accounts. The storekeeper before him had been very dishonest with the money, but Nanak was different. He kept the accounts very well. The Khan Sahib was delighted with his work and his sister hoped that Nanak would change and become a good, hard-working husband too.

But although Nanak did his work well, he was not happy. He had a Muslim servant, Mardana, who could play on a musical instrument called the *rabab*. So every evening Nanak and the servant would sit together and sing hymns. Every morning Nanak would get up early and sing hymns again, and then go for his work.

Mardana on the rabab

Though he worked hard he would often say to himself, 'What is the use of this work? Why should I work for Khan Sahib when I can easily work for God?'

Finally one night, as he worked till quite late, Nanak suddenly stopped. 'This is all a waste!' He cried, throwing his pen down on the ground. 'Shall I spend all my life doing these **wretched** accounts?'

The next day Nanak gave up his work and joined a band of holy men who wandered from place to place. He gave away all his money, and everything he had. He gave away all his clothes and kept only one piece of cloth to cover himself. He took with him a bowl so that he could beg for his food, a strong stick to help him on his journey and a small mat on which he could sit and say his prayers.

Nanak wandered from place to place, all over North India. He went on pilgrimage to both Muslim and Hindu religious places. He talked to the Muslims and to the Hindus. He did not like many of the customs of the Hindus or the Muslims.

'God belongs to us all,' he would say. 'You will not find God only in your mosque or in the temple. You will only find God in your own heart.'

One day Nanak and his servant came to Haridwar where there was a great festival going on. There were many people taking a holy bath in the sacred waters of the river Ganga. They stood in the river, took water in their hands and poured it out, facing the east. Nanak, who stood watching for some time, put down his bowl and stick on the river bank and entered the water. He too took water in his hands, but instead of throwing it towards the east he threw it towards the west. Seeing him do this, the Hindus were amazed, and they cried, 'Are you a fool? Why are you throwing the water in that direction?'

'Why are you throwing it to the east?' asked Nanak.

'Don't you know?' asked the Hindus. 'We are offering it to our **ancestors**.'

'And where are they?' asked Nanak.

'Where? In heaven, of course.'

'And how far is heaven?' asked Nanak quietly.

'Many, many miles away,' replied the Hindus. 'But you have not answered our question. Why are you throwing the water towards the west?'

'Oh,' said Nanak. 'You see, I have some fields near Lahore. The rains have been bad this year. I am throwing water on to my fields.'

Guru Nanak offering water

'How will the water from here reach Lahore?'

'How will the water from here reach your ancestors?' asked Nanak. This made the people stop and think.

Slowly people began to listen to Nanak's teachings. He went from place to place and many people followed him and became his disciples. He travelled all over North India and then went down to South India, and even as far as Ceylon.

Once while he was on a pilgrimage, Nanak stopped one night at a mosque. He went to sleep with his feet turned towards Mecca. Early in the morning, a Muslim priest came to the mosque and found Nanak asleep. He was horrified to see that his feet were turned towards Mecca. He caught hold of Nanak's arm and pulled him awake.

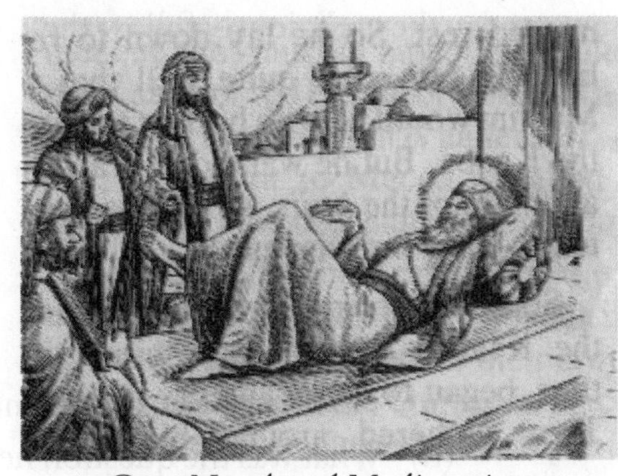
Guru Nanak and Muslim priests

'What is the matter?' cried Nanak. 'What's happened?'

'Have you no sense?' shouted the priest. 'Do you sleep with your feet turned towards God?'

Nanak sat up. 'God is everywhere. Please turn my feet in the direction where there is no God.' The Muslim priest had no answer.

Did you know?

The Golden Temple or the Harmandir Sahib Temple in Amritsar is the most important shrine of the Sikhs. Its construction began in 1588 and was completed in 1601.

The period of travelling probably ended in 1520 CE. It seems that Guru Nanak saw Babur's attack on India. After the Guru's travels had ended, a wealthy follower gave him some land on the bank of the river Ravi. There the village of Kartarpur was built and Guru Nanak spent the rest of his life there.

The Golden Temple, Amritsar

Nanak died in 1539 CE. His ideas were written down after his death in a book called *Adi Granth,* which is the holy book of the Sikhs. Later on, the Sikhs became a powerful community, and even today they religiously follow the gentle teachings of Nanak.

Exercises

1. **Answer the following.**
   (a) How was Nanak different from the other children?
   (b) What was the question he asked his teacher? What did the teacher say?

(c) Why did he give the shopping money to the gypsies?
(d) Why did Nanak give up his job?
(e) Why was the Muslim priest not able to tell Nanak which way he should turn his feet?

2. **Fill in the blanks.**
(a) Guru Nanak was the first of the .... Sikh gurus.
(b) Though he was a very intelligent boy Nanak was also a great ....
(c) Nanak worked as a storekeeper in a town called ....
(d) Nanak's companion and devoted servant, Mardana, played a musical instrument called ....

3. **Say whether the following are True or False.**
(a) Every morning and evening Nanak would spend his time in singing hymns.
(b) Nanak died in 1559 CE.
(c) Nanak's teachings and ideas were written down in a book called the *Adi Granth.*
(d) Nanak learnt Persian from the Sultan of Persia.
(e) The Sikh temple is called a gurudwara.

Things to do

1. **For your scrapbook!**
Collect a picture of a gurudwara and stick it in your book. Try and find out the names of the ten Sikh Gurus.

2. **Find out.**
Try and visit a gurudwara and find out about the community meals called *langar*.

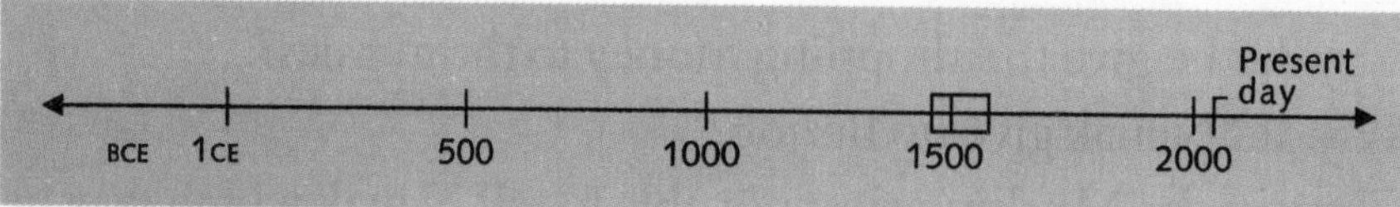

Michelangelo
—The famous sculptor

You have read about Leonardo da Vin\ci in an earlier chapter. In this chapter we will read about another great artist of this period—Michelangelo. He was a great sculptor and painter from Florence, and lived about the same time as Leonardo da Vinci.

Five hundred years ago, just outside a town called Florence in Italy, a boy was playing in a stone **quarry**. Great blocks of stone lay all around him. Workmen shouted as they used ropes to pull the huge blocks on to carts. The little boy had a hammer and a **chisel** in his hand, and he was **chipping** away at a block of stone on the ground in front of him. The boy's name was Michelangelo, and his father, who worked in the stone quarry, did not know that his son would one day be one of the most famous sculptors or stone carvers in the world.

Words to remember

quarry : a place where stone, slate etc. is dug out of the ground.

chisel : a tool for shaping wood, stone or metal.

chipping : breaking off small pieces from something.

public : of or concerning people in general.

statue : a figure of a person, an animal, etc. in stone, metal, etc. usually the same size as in real life or larger.

bravo : well done.

design : a plan or sketch of something to be made.

One day, his father said to him, 'Your brothers are all at school, Michelangelo. It is time you were at school, too.'

'I don't want to go to school, Father,' said the boy. 'I want to make things out of stone.'

'You must go to school,' said his father. 'You have to learn to read and write.'

'I can draw, father,' said Michelangelo. 'Isn't that better than reading and writing?'

'No, it isn't. Tomorrow you are going to school with your brothers.'

Michelangelo

Michelangelo was not interested in school subjects. He hardly ever listened to what the teacher said. Whenever the teacher asked him a question, he would look down and think. He would never know the answer because he would not study his lessons. He was always drawing pictures. His teacher would scold him, his father and mother would scold him, and they would often beat him too, but Michelangelo would not listen. At last his father realized that the boy was not going to study. When he was thirteen years old, his father sent him to work with two brothers who were painters. After a year, the ruler of the state of Florence opened a school for boys who wanted to learn sculpture, and Michelangelo was sent there. He was paid a small salary every month. Michelangelo was so clever at his work that the other boys in the school were jealous of him. One boy, whose name was Torrignano, was bigger than Michelangelo and he was always teasing him.

'Your head is like a block of stone,' he used to shout. 'You will never be a sculptor. Why don't you leave this school and go and break stones for the road? Nobody will want even those!'

One day Michelangelo could stand the teasing no longer. He sprang at Torrignano and soon a terrible fight took place. Michelangelo fought like a tiger, but Torrignano was bigger and heavier. At last he landed a crashing blow on Michelangelo's nose and broke it. That broken nose reminded Michelangelo of the fight for the rest of his life.

When the ruler of Florence died in 1492 CE, the school was closed down and Michelangelo had to leave school and wander from town to town. His carving was so good that soon his name became well known. People asked him to carve statues for them, for their **public** buildings and palaces.

One day Michelangelo came back to Florence. Outside the Cathedral, there was a huge block of stone, which weighed about eight thousand kilograms. It had been lying there for many years because no sculptor was brave enough to start working on it. Michelangelo looked at the stone and thought what a fine **statue** it would make. He started working on it and began to carve the figure of David, a famous character from the Bible. After a great deal of labour, it was finished and the Mayor of the town came, with a great crowd of people, to inspect the statue. Michelangelo, who knew the Mayor too well, was sure that he would find some fault with his work. When the cover was taken off the statue, all the people in the crowd were amazed.

'**Bravo**!' they shouted. 'A masterpiece!'

Then the Mayor stepped forward.

'It is good, Michelangelo,' he said. 'Very good indeed. But I have one thing to say. That nose,' he said, looking carefully at the statue, 'that nose is a little too thick, I think.'

David

Michelangelo was angry at this, but he asked the Mayor to look again more carefully. While the Mayor was looking at the statue, Michelangelo quietly picked up a handful of stone dust and chips from the pile at the foot of the statue.

'Yes, yes,' cried the Mayor. 'I have looked at it most carefully. The nose is too thick.'

'I am sure you are right, your Honour,' said Michelangelo. 'I shall take a little bit off.'

He climbed up on the wooden poles at the side of the statue and pretended to chip away some stone from the nose with his hammer and chisel. As he did so, he let fall some of the dust and chips which he had taken up from the ground. After ten minute's work he climbed down. He had not chipped away any stone from the nose at all.

'How is that, your Honour?' he asked the Mayor.

'Perfect!' said the Mayor. 'I knew it was too thick.'

Michelangelo next worked for a long time on a huge statue of Moses, another figure from the Bible. This is one of the greatest works of sculpture in the world. They say that even Michelangelo himself was delighted with the statue because it looked so lifelike. While working on it for months, he was very happy, slowly watching it take shape. At last when it was finished, Michelangelo looked up at the huge figure and said to himself, 'This is not stone, this is Moses.'

The statue of Moses

He looked at the statue for a long time and then he cried out, 'Why don't you speak?'

Moses remained silent.

'Moses!' cried Michelangelo, 'Why don't you speak?'

Michelangelo was so angry at the statue's silence that he struck it a great blow on the knee with his hammer. The mark of his blow can still be seen today.

A few years later, the Pope called Michelangelo. There was a famous chapel in Rome called the Sistine Chapel. It was 400 feet long, and the Pope wanted to decorate it. He wanted a beautiful painting to cover the whole ceiling! He wanted it to show the whole story of man and God.

The years that followed were very difficult for Michelangelo. He had to build a huge framework of wood. All the painting had to be done while he was lying on his back. As you can imagine, it was most uncomfortable. His limbs ached. The paint fell on his clothes and into his eyes. Every month or so, the Pope would come and stand at the bottom of the wooden frame to watch his paintings. At last the painting was finished. It is still one of the greatest paintings the world has ever seen.

The story of man and god from the Sistine Chapel

Then the Pope wanted another painting, this time on the walls of the chapel. The subject was 'The Last Judgement'. This showed Christ sending all the sinners to hell. The work was finished in six years. When it was nearly finished, one of the Pope's officials came to see the painting. He looked at it for a long time and then told Michelangelo, 'Your work is wonderful, but it is quite the wrong subject for a church. It will stop people from praying.'

Did you know?

Over the 500 years or so since painted, the ceiling of the Sistine Chapel had become dirty. It took a team of skilled experts twelve years from 1980–1992 CE to remove the dirt without damaging the painting!

Michelangelo was angry. As soon as the official had left, he took his paints and skilfully painted the picture of the official. Then he added horns and a snake round his body and made him into a devil!

St Peter's Basilica

He **designed** the dome of a huge church in Rome called St Peter's Basilica. He also wrote a great deal of poetry. Although he had been very bad-tempered in his youth, he became gentler as he grew older.

Michelangelo continued to paint and work until he died in 1564 CE, just before he reached the age of eighty-nine.

Exercises

1. **Answer the following.**
   (a) Why did Michelangelo have to leave school?
   (b) How did Michelangelo show that the Mayor was a fool and that he criticized everything to show others how clever he was?
   (c) Why did Michelangelo hit the statue of Moses?
   (d) Describe how Michelangelo painted the ceiling of the Sistine Chapel.
   (e) What did Michelangelo depict in his painting, 'The Last Judgement'?

2. **Fill in the blanks.**
   (a) Michelangelo's father worked in a ....
   (b) The ruler of .... opened a school for boys who wanted to learn ....
   (c) Michelangelo's nose was broken by ....
   (d) Michelangelo went to a school for sculptors in the town of ....
   (e) Michelangelo designed the dome of the church in Rome called ....

3. **Say whether the following are True or False.**
   (a) The famous chapel in Rome was called Sistine Chapel.
   (b) Michelangelo died at the age of eighty.
   (c) The Mayor liked the work of Michelangelo and did not find any fault with the statue of David.
   (d) Michelangelo had left painting in his old age.

Things to do

1. **Become an artist.**
   Take a piece of soap or plasticine and try to carve a figure or the head of a person or an animal out of it. You may use a penknife or a sharp piece of stick.

2. **Observe.**
   Examine a stone statue in your school, or some park or a museum. Feel it with your hands and see if you can feel the mark of the chisel on it.

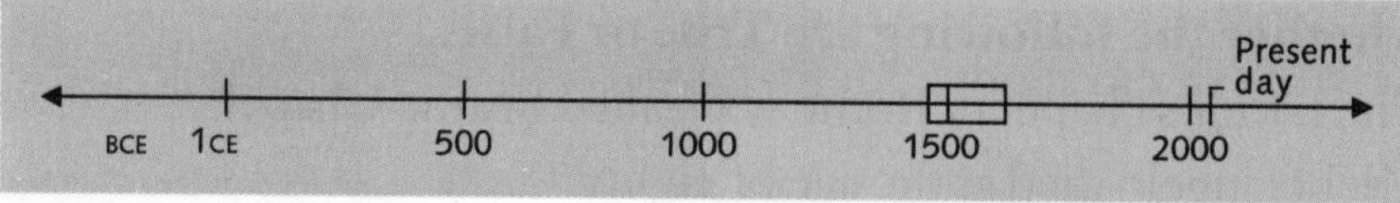

12

Babur

—The first Mughal

You have already read in Chapter 4 about the Mongols. In the early sixteenth century, Babur, a **descendant** of two great Mongol conquerors, Timur and Chengiz Khan, rose to power. The empire that he founded was known as the Mughal (a Persian word for Mongol) Empire.

Zahir-ud-din Muhammad was born in 1483 CE, and from an early age he was given the name of Babur, which means 'the Tiger'. His home was in the country of valleys and mountains—Farghana in Central Asia. Babur's uncle was the king

Babur

Words to remember

descendant of : (here) born in the family of.
expedition : journey for a definite purpose.
orchards : fruit gardens.
memoirs : story of one's own life.
hospitable : giving or likely to give warm welcome.
pomegranate : thick-skinned round fruit which when ripe, has a reddish centre full of seeds.
polo : ball game played on horseback with a kind of stick.
trenches : ditches dug in the ground.
administrator : a person with an ability to organize.

of Samarkand. Babur spent his early days in the midst of a wild and beautiful country. He learnt to ride and to shoot with a bow and arrow. He learnt to climb mountains and to swim in the ice-cold streams.

When his father died in 1494 CE, Babur was only eleven years old. As soon as the old sheikh died, Babur's cousins and uncles turned against him and he had to run away. He returned three years later and took the city of Samarkand. But one day, while he was out on an **expedition**, his enemies won back the city. Again he went on his wanderings in the mountains, and slowly collected a small band of followers. In 1500 CE, with a small number of men, he attacked Samarkand again. The city had a wall all around and enormous gates. Some of his men climbed the wall and opened the gates; then Babur and his men burst into the city. It was early morning and most people were asleep. They woke up when Babur entered, and rejoiced; they were happy to see the boy again. Babur loved Samarkand. It was a beautiful place, with fine **orchards** and gardens, and had a magnificent palace.

A painting showing Babur planning a garden

Babur did not reign long on the throne of Samarkand. The next year, a famous Khan attacked the city. Babur defended it bravely, but at last there was no food left and once again he had to flee to the open countryside. He was again a wanderer without a home.

Babur enjoyed his life in the countryside with his small band of soldiers. He described some of the pleasures of his life in his **memoirs**. As he wandered about through the mountains and valleys, Babur spent many nights in villages. The villagers were very kind and **hospitable** to him and his followers. At one village, he met an old lady who was a hundred and eleven years old. She remembered talking to the soldiers of his great-grandfather, Timur of

Samarkand, when they attacked India in 1398 CE. Babur listened with great interest to the stories the old lady told him. Perhaps at that moment was born the idea of invading India.

Babur spent his days in fighting and often tried to attack Samarkand. But at last, he gave up the idea of conquering Samarkand and began to look towards the south, to Kabul, where one of his uncles had once ruled. He attacked it and entered the city in 1504 CE.

Kabul was a beautiful city with fine gardens and lots of fruit—oranges, **pomegranates** and melons. Babur spent his time playing **polo**, hunting or fighting. When he had time, he designed and built more gardens.

In 1525 CE, Babur set out to attack India. He had only about 12,000 men with him but he had been promised help by Daulat Khan, the governor of Punjab. They marched together against Ibrahim Lodi, who at that time was the Sultan of Delhi. When Babur reached India, Daulat was afraid to help him, and Babur started off to Delhi by himself with his small army of men.

A painting depicting the Battle of Panipat

Ibrahim Lodi was reported to have 100,000 men and 100 elephants. But Babur had something which Ibrahim did not have—guns. There were hardly any guns at that time in India and Babur had managed to find guns at Kabul. He had some cannons and some rifles as well.

The two armies met at a place called Panipat, a small village near Delhi. Both armies remained in position opposite each other for a week before the battle began. Babur was an excellent general and he planned the battle very carefully. He collected 600–700 country bullock carts from the surrounding countryside.

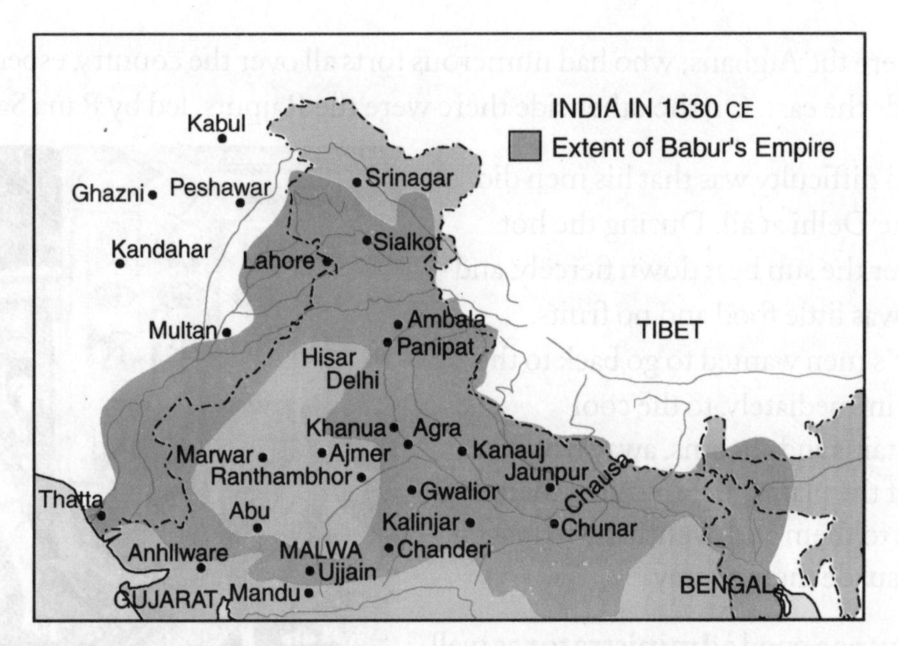

He placed these in front of his guns, but was careful to leave spaces between each group of carts so that his cavalry could get through. On his right side, was the town of Panipat. On his left side, he dug deep **trenches** and filled the spaces between them with tree trunks and branches. In this way, he hoped that the enemy would be unable to attack him either from the right or the left. As soon as the battle began, Babur sent two small forces to attack the enemy, one on the right and one on the left. Then he used his guns to fire on the enemy at the centre. Finally his cavalry charged. Huge numbers of enemy soldiers were killed and the elephants were of no use to them, because the guns frightened them and they ran about in every direction. About 15,000 of the enemy were killed, including their commander, Ibrahim Lodi.

After the battle, Babur's son Humayun was sent to capture Agra. When Humayun reached Agra, he was presented the famous Koh-i-noor diamond by the Raja of Gwalior. When Babur arrived at the head of his army, Humayun gave the diamond to Babur. Before the enemy could recover from its defeat, Delhi was taken.

Although Babur had taken Delhi, he had not by any means taken the whole of India— there were two dangerous enemies still fighting against him. On one side were the Afghans, who had numerous forts all over the country, especially towards the east. On the other side there were the Rajputs, led by Rana Sanga.

A third difficulty was that his men did not like Delhi at all. During the hot weather the sun beat down fiercely, and there was little food and no fruits. Babur's men wanted to go back to the north immediately, to the cool mountains and streams, away from the heat of the plains. Babur called them and talked to them and eventually managed to persuade them to stay.

Babur in his court

Babur was a good **administrator** as well as a good general. He allowed his officers to go into the country and to take over districts which were in the hands of the Afghans. His men went everywhere, taking towns and forts, and his empire stretched farther and farther.

But now the Rajputs under Rana Sanga began to attack him. The Rana was old and had fought in more than a hundred battles. His body was scarred with more than eighty wounds and he had lost one eye and one arm. The Rana had over a 100,000 men and Babur had only 10,000. Babur advanced to a place called Khanua and spent a number of days getting ready for the battle. He followed the same plan that he had once used at Panipat. The men were busy all day, but when they got the news that the Afghans had taken some of Babur's forts, they became disheartened and Babur was afraid that they might lose the battle. Babur, although a Muslim, had always been a heavy drinker of wine. Before the battle began, all his drinking cups, beautiful gold and silver vessels, were carried to the battlefield. Babur broke them to pieces with his own hands.

'I shall never drink again,' he told them. 'You can be sure that we shall win this battle.'

The next morning, the Rajputs attacked. Line upon line of Rajputs galloped towards Babur's guns, but most of them were killed. Then Babur sent out his cavalry on both sides and the battle was soon won by him.

Babur's kingdom now stretched far and wide. He ruled the country well. He gave a number of districts to his officers, and they had to pay taxes to the emperor's treasure house. Babur employed hundreds of men to build a fine capital city at Agra. He played polo, went hunting and wrote beautiful poetry in Persian, and at the same time he was constantly busy looking after the affairs of his empire. He was a wise and just emperor, and although he was sometimes cruel, it was usually for a good reason.

Did you know?

Baburnama **is the autobiography of Babur which gives a detailed glimpse of his life and times. It is written in Chagatai, the spoken language of the Timurids.**

One day Humayun, Babur's favourite son, became ill. In spite of all help from the doctors he did not get well. Babur was heartbroken. He was then told by one of the wise men to offer God the most precious thing he had. To this he said, 'What could be more precious to me than my own life?' Next he walked three times round the bed of his son saying. 'O God! If a life can be given for another life, I, Babur, give my life for my son Humayun.' After this Humayun soon became well but Babur became ill and died shortly afterwards, leaving his vast empire to Humayun.

Babur was the first of a line of famous emperors called the Mughals who created one of the greatest empires that India has ever known.

Exercises

1. **Answer the following.**
   (a) Why did Babur invade India?

(b) Discuss why the following places were important in Babur's life:
Samarkand; Khanua; Panipat; Agra;

(c) Why did Babur break all his drinking cups and vessels?

(d) Describe the personal traits of Babur.

(e) Why do you think Babur was a loving father?

2. Fill in the blanks.

(a) In 1504 CE, Babur became the king of.........................

(b) In 1525 CE, Babur set out to attack........................... .

(c) After defeating Ibrahim Lodi, Babur sent his son
.... to ....

(d) Babur's son presented him with a magnificent .... called the ....

(e) Babur's capital city was called..........................

3. Match the following.

(a) Ibrahim Lodi	Rajput ruler
(b) Daulat Khan	Sultan of Delhi
(c) Rana Sanga	The first Mughal ruler
(d) Babur	Governor of Punjab

Things to do

1. Become a historian!

Each one of you should write a report on what happened yesterday in school or in your class or even at home. Read out the reports in class.

2. Find out.

What is polo? Try to find out how it is played and write a few lines about it.

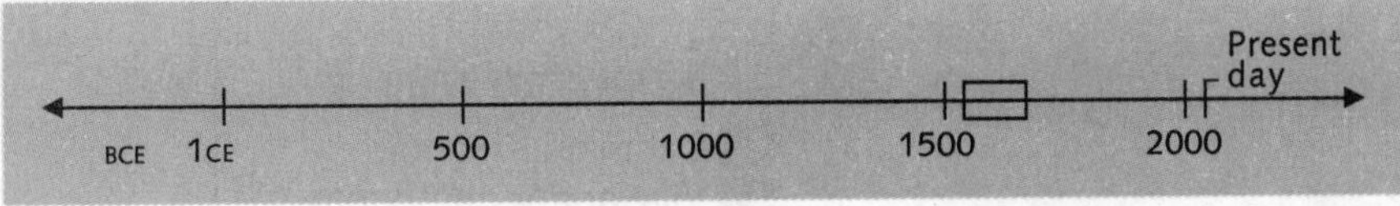

Sri Krishna Deva Raya

—The great king of the Deccan

13

The kingdom of Vijayanagar was founded by two brothers, Harihara and Bukka in 1336 CE. It had a long line of able rulers who made it into a powerful state. But one ruler, Krishna Deva Raya, has made a special name for himself in the history of Vijayanagar. Under him the kingdom became the most powerful state in South India. His empire extended over the present-day Andhra Pradesh and Karnataka. Much of our information about his reign comes from the accounts of two Portuguese travellers, Domingo Paes and Nuniz.

When Krishna Deva Raya became the king of Vijayanagar in 1509 CE, the empire was in great **turmoil**. There were uprisings in different parts of the empire, which posed a great challenge to the new ruler. He **subdued** the rebellious chiefs through a series of attacks on their territories. Then he decided to try and control his powerful enemy, Gajapathi of Orissa, who had fully occupied the east coast, parts of which were earlier in the Vijayanagar empire.

Words to remember

turmoil : a state of confusion and uncertainty.
subdued : to bring something under control by using force.
flourishing : to develop quickly.
siege : a military operation in which an army surrounds a place and cuts off all outside access to force surrender.
pious : religious; holy.
staunch : strong and loyal in one's opinions and attitude.

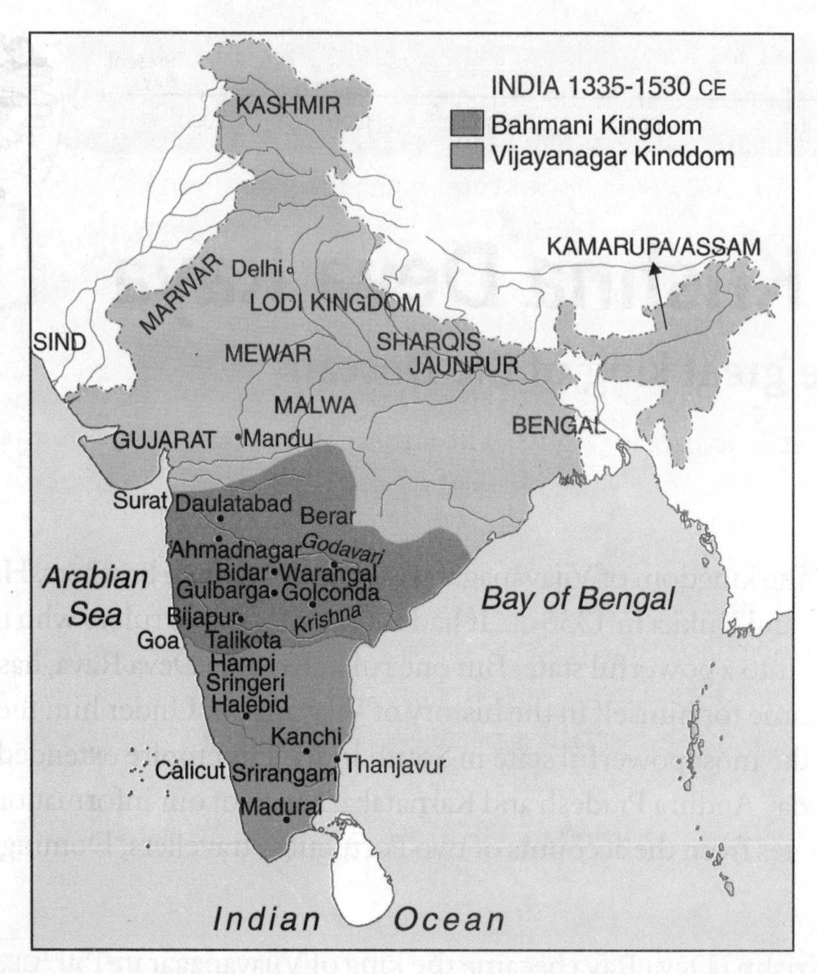

The Gajapathi had strong fortresses and a large army supported by thousands of elephants. He also had the support of his Muslim friends, the rulers of Bijapur and Golconda. One by one, Krishna Deva Raya captured the forts of Udayagiri, Kondavidu, Kondapalli and the coastal parts of Telangana that originally belonged to the Vijayanagar kingdom.

His conquests against enemy rulers continued and in 1520 CE, he captured the fortress of Raichur from Ismail Adil Shah of Bijapur after a difficult **siege** during which 16,000 Vijayanagar soldiers were killed. During this campaign 703,000 foot soldiers, 32,600 cavalry and 551 elephants were used. In his last battle, he completely destroyed the fortress of Gulbarga, the early capital of the Bahmani Sultanate.

Domingo Paes, a Portuguese merchant who lived in Vijayanagar city (1520–22 CE) described the Emperor in these words: '... He is the most feared and perfect king that could possibly be, cheerful of disposition and very merry, he is one that seeks to honour foreigners, receives them kindly.... He is a great ruler and a man of much justice....'. Paes considered Vijayanagar to be 'the best provided city in the world' with a population of not less than a half a million and estimated the city to be at least as large as Rome.

Krishna Deva Raya was a great statesman and under his rule the Vijayanagar empire reached great heights. The empire was divided into a number of provinces often under members of the royal family. The provinces were divided into further subdivisions.

Under Krishna Deva Raya, Vijayanagar became very rich. Paes was stunned by the wealth and he remarks in his account 'to try and tell all of what I saw is hopeless, for I went along with my head so often turned from one side to the other that I was almost falling backward off my horse with my senses lost. The cost of it all is not so much to be wondered at, as there is so much money in the land, and the chiefs are so wealthy.'

The ruins at Hampi, the capital of Vijayanagar

During Krishna Deva Raya's reign art and culture flourished. Many Telugu, Sanskrit, and Kannada poets enjoyed the patronage of the emperor. In his palace, a separate hall used for literary gatherings, had eight poets, known as *Ashta Diggajalu* or the eight pillars. Valuable contributions were made to Sanskrit, Telugu, Kannada and Tamil literature during his rule and it was rightly called the 'golden age of Telugu literature'. His most famous piece of writing in Telugu, *Amukta Malyada*, which deals with administration, is considered as a great work in Telugu literature. He was also well versed in Kannada, Tamil and Sanskrit languages. He was also a great lover of music and was himself an excellent veena player.

Krishna Deva Raya established friendly relations with the Portuguese, who set up the Portuguese Dominion of India in Goa in 1510 CE. The Emperor obtained guns and Arabian horses from the Portuguese merchants. He also used Portuguese expertise in improving the water supply to Vijayanagar city.

The Vitthala temple

Deva Raya was a **pious** Hindu and visited holy shrines and made generous gifts to them even while he was engaged in military operations. Though he was a **staunch** Vaishnavite, he respected all faiths.

The Vitthala and Virupaksha temples are fine examples of architecture of this period.

Did you know?

Tenali Rama, one of the most popular folk figures, was a jester in the court of Krishna Deva Raya. Known for his sharp wit and sense of humour, he was one of the eight pillars in the Vijayanagar court.

During his reign there was perfect understanding among different religions. Muslims and Christians were allowed freedom of worship and could build mosques and churches.

The Virupaksha temple

Hampi was the capital of Krishna Deva Raya and the remains tell us that it must have been truly a city of victory as its name signifies. Paes and Nuniz describe Hampi bazaar: 'In this street lived many merchants and there you will find all sorts of rubies, and diamonds, and emeralds, and pearls, and seed pearls, and cloths, and every sort of thing there is on earth and that you may wish to buy.'

However, the glorious rule of Krishna Deva Raya came to an end with his death in 1530 CE. Thirty years after his death, the Bahmani sultans united and carefully planned the battle of Talikota, which they won and finally defeated the Vijayanagar rulers.

Exercises

1. **Answer the following.**
   (a) What were the challenges faced by Krishna Deva Raya when he became the king in 1509 CE ?
   (b) How did Paes describe the emperor?
   (c) What does Paes write about the market of Hampi?
   (d) How did Krishna Deva Raya gain from Portuguese friendship?

2. **Fill in the blanks.**
   (a) Krishna Deva Raya's empire extended over the present-day .... and ....

(b) Deva Raya's magnum opus in Telugu, is ……………….

(c) Deva Raya's most powerful enemy was ……………………

(d) In Deva Raya's palace, a separate hall used for literary gatherings, had eight poets, known as ……………….

(e) Much of our information about his reign comes from the accounts of………………….. and ……………..

3. Say whether the following are True or False.

(a) The Gajapathi had strong fortresses and a large army supported by thousands of horses.

(b) Krishna Deva Raya obtained guns and Arabian horses from the Arabian merchants.

(c) Deva Raya was an excellent veena player.

(d) Krishna Deva Raya did not allow Muslims and Christians freedom of worship.

Things to do

1. Do a storytelling session.

Tenali Rama was a court jester of Krishna Deva Raya. He had a brilliant sense of humour. Today, his tales have become a legend. Read some of Tenali Rama's tales and narrate them in the storytelling session of your class.

2. World Heritage Monuments.

The United Nations Educational, Scientific and Cultural Organization or the UNESCO has listed some monuments as World Heritage Sites which must be preserved and protected. These sites may be forests, mountain ranges, lakes, deserts, buildings, complexes or cities. Hampi, the capital of Krishna Deva Raya is one such site. There are many other places in India that come under this list. Find out about these World Heritage sites in India.

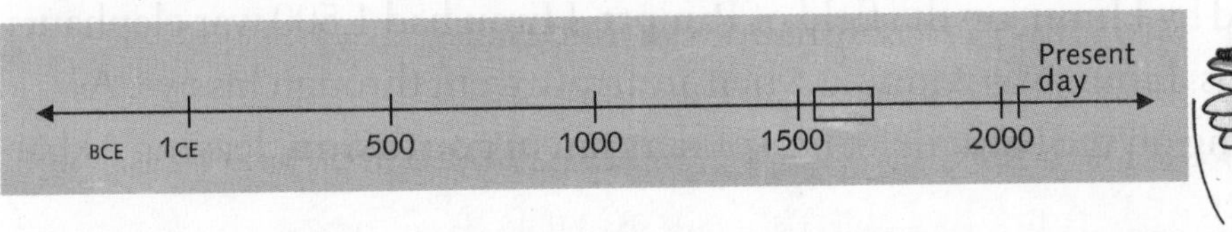

14

Akbar
—The great liberal Mughal

You have read in Chapter 12 about Babur, who was the first Mughal emperor of India. His grandson, Akbar, was born in 1542 CE. He is probably one of the greatest rulers of India. He lost his father, Humayun, when he was only a boy of thirteen. The young Akbar was hurriedly placed on the throne. He was strong, well built, good at wrestling, riding and hunting. The kingdom already stretched from Afghanistan to Delhi and Agra. Akbar was still too young to rule such a large kingdom all by himself. Bairam Khan, a friend of his father, became his guardian and advisor.

Akbar

Before Akbar's position could be safe, he had to fight many people. A very able general called Himu controlled large areas of North India. In CE 1556, soon after he came to power, Akbar faced a

Words to remember

confusion : disorder

foster brother : when someone is brought up by someone else's parents, he is a foster brother to their children.

laid siege : surrounded a place by army to keep people or goods from entering or leaving the place.

large army, led by Himu, on the field of Panipat. Himu had 1,500 war elephants and many guns. Himu was winning when an arrow went through his eye. As Himu lay dying on the battlefield, his soldiers ran in **confusion**, leaving Akbar an easy winner.

The victory at Panipat gave Akbar greater confidence. He now refused to be guided and controlled by Bairam Khan. When Akbar was seventeen, he dismissed Bairam Khan and sent him off to Mecca. He took charge of the kingdom himself. But he found it really hard to make his nobles obey him. Adham Khan, his **foster brother**, would not listen to him. When Adham Khan murdered Akbar's chief minister right in the palace, Akbar could not bear it any longer. He had Adham Khan thrown down from the roof of the palace. At nineteen, Akbar was determined to be the master.

Once he became the real ruler of the empire, he turned to the areas still lying beyond his kingdom. The brave Rajput kings had lost to Babur, but they still remained a proud race. Akbar tried to make friends with the Rajput kings. The first Rajput king to accept Akbar's offer of friendship was Raja Bihari Mal of Amber. Akbar married his daughter, and made his grandson, Man Singh, a general in the army.

A painting showing the attack on Chittor

But other Rajput kings refused to submit to Akbar. These kings were led by Rana Udai Singh of Mewar. In 1567 CE, Akbar **laid siege** to the great fortress of Chittor. Udai Singh escaped into the hills, leaving his brave general, Jaimal, to defend the city. Jaimal and his soldiers resisted Akbar's army for four months. But at last Akbar managed to kill

Jaimal with a lucky shot from his gun. The Rajput soldiers came out of the fort, and fought for every house, for every foot of ground until they were all killed. The women burnt themselves to death.

Udai Singh took shelter in the forests around the Aravalli Hills. He founded a new city called Udaipur on a large lake called Udai Sagar. Mewar still refused to accept Akbar as their emperor. But the other Rajput chiefs surrendered one by one.

Udai Singh died in 1572 CE. His brave son, Pratap Singh, became the new king. He lived in the forests, and vowed to sleep out in the open on beds of straw, not to touch his dishes of gold and silver, eat only wild fruits from trees, and not to shave his beard, till Chittor was freed. In 1576 CE, Akbar sent his Rajput general, Man Singh, to punish Rana Pratap. A furious battle was fought at the mountain pass of Haldighati. The Rajputs fought bravely, but Pratap was defeated.

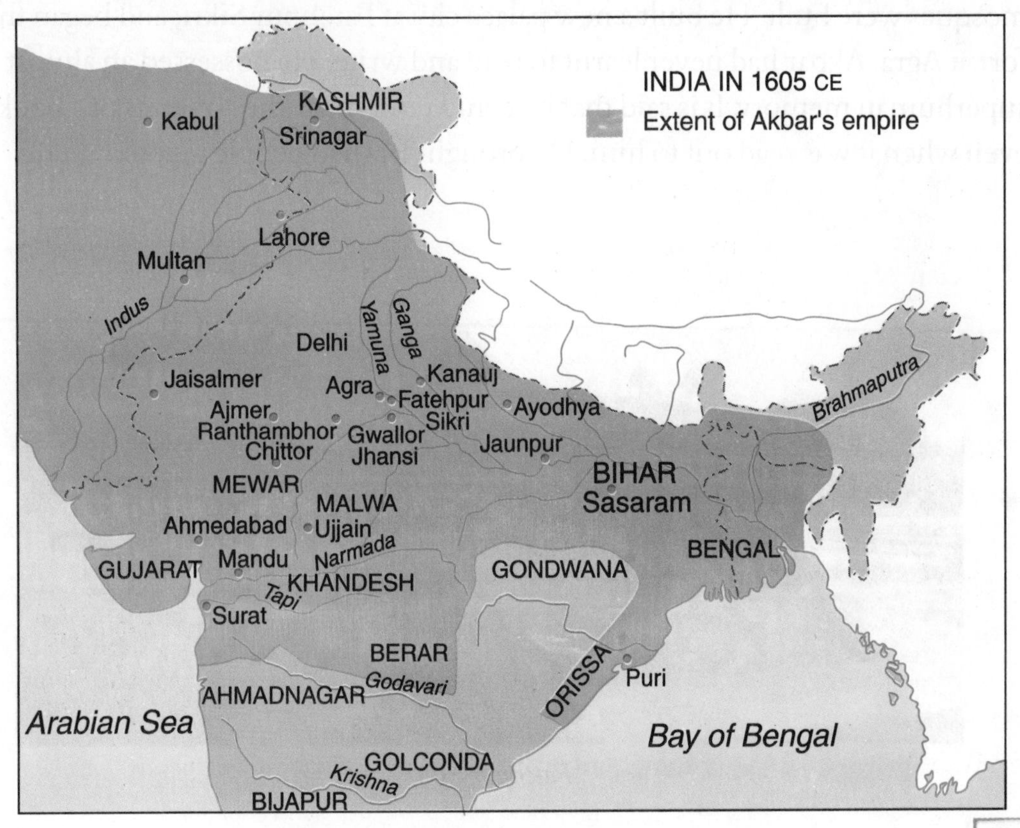

Akbar conquered the whole of northern, eastern and western India by 1595 CE. His empire was by then the size of Europe.

Akbar knew that winning battles did not mean much if he could not keep his people happy. He set down the laws very carefully, and had an able group of ministers to help him maintain justice. The empire was divided into *subas* or districts, with a *subedar* in charge of every district. Akbar organized his nobles and army under the Mansabdari System. Under this each official was given a rank called a **mansab**. The word mansab means office and the officers were called mansabdars. Each mansabdar had a certain number of men under him. He had to maintain a fixed number of horses, elephants and carts according to his rank. This system worked well and continued without much change for almost two hundred years.

Akbar loved fine buildings. During his time, many splendid temples and mosques were built. He built a new palace city at Fatehpur Sikri, and began the fort at Agra. Akbar had never learnt to read and write. He possessed an almost superhuman memory. It is said that he could remember the contents of a book even when it was read out to him. He brought learned people together in his

Fatehpur Sikri

court, and learnt a lot as he listened to them speaking or discussing. He loved painting and took lessons in drawing. He studied geography and loved to meet travellers. He was always surrounded by learned people and his court was famous for the *Navratna* or nine gems.

Akbar in discussion with people from other religions

Akbar himself was a Muslim, but he was fair to other religions. When he found people from different religions fighting with one another, he introduced a new religion called the *Din-i-Illahi*.

It had the best of all the religions Akbar knew. Akbar did not force his people to follow the new religion. Though the new religion never became popular, Akbar proved that people could live together as one with tolerance. The new religion failed because it was much ahead of the times. A Christian missionary wrote about Akbar, 'Indeed he was a great king for he knew that a good ruler is he who can command simultaneously, the obedience, respect, love and fear of his subjects.' People often say that Akbar lived much ahead of his times.

Did you know?

Emperor Akbar wanted a son and so he went to visit Salim Chisti. The wise man told Akbar that he would soon have a son. A year later, the queen had a son. Akbar built Fatehpur Sikri to honour him.

Akbar's last few years were unhappy. His son, Salim, turned against him, and set up his own royal court at Allahabad. Akbar's other two sons were already dead. Before his death in 1605 CE, Akbar forgave Salim and named him the next emperor. Salim came to be known as Emperor Jahangir.

Akbar's tomb at Sikandra

Exercises

1. **Answer the following.**
   (a) How did Akbar win against Himu?
   (b) Describe how the Rajputs fought for Chittor.
   (c) What happened at Haldighati?
   (d) What was the Din-i-Ilahi?
   (e) What do you know about the following?
   Adham Khan, Raja Bihari Mal, Man Singh, Bairam Khan, Jaimal

2. **Fill in the blanks.**
   (a) Akbar was the grandson of .... and the son of ....
   (b) Akbar became king at the age of ....

(c) Akbar's empire was divided into .... or ...., with a .... in charge of each of them.

(d) Akbar built a new city at ....

(e) Akbar forgave .... and named him the next emperor.

3. Match the following.

(a) New religion	Bairam Khan
(b) Akbar's guardian	Din-i-Illahi
(c) Jaimal	District
(d) *Suba*	Udai Singh's brave general

Things to do

1. Map work.

Draw or trace a map of India and mark the cities of Chittor, Udaipur and Agra on it.

2. Find out.

(a) Try to find the names of any four buildings present in Fatehpur Sikri. Write a few sentences about each of them. Also find out the names of the nine gems present in the court of Akbar.

(b) Birbal was one of the 'Nine Gems' at Akbar's court. Birbal was known for his wit and wisdom. Akbar and Birbal's stories are very famous. Visit the following website for some of these stories.
http://www.telugutoranam.com/kids/akbar.html
(accessed on 14 August 2006)

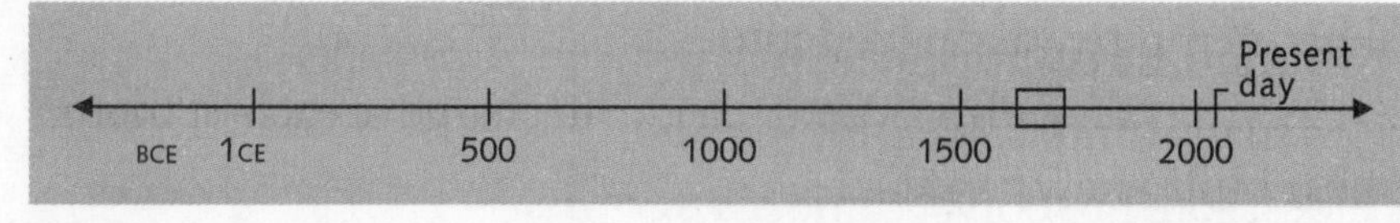

15

Shah Jahan

—The emperor who built the Taj Mahal

Shah Jahan was the fifth Mughal emperor who ruled India from 1628–58 CE. He was the third son of Emperor Jahangir, and the grandson of Emperor Akbar about whom you have read in the last chapter. He was born in Lahore in the year 1592 CE and was called Prince Khurram in his early years. Under his rule, the Mughal empire reached its greatest **prosperity**.

Shah Jahan

Words to remember

prosperity : state of well-being and having lots of wealth.

conspiracies : secret plans to commit a crime or do harm.

commissioned : made a formal request to somebody to design or create a piece of work

calligrapher : the person who knows the art of beautiful handwriting

magnificence : the state of being very attractive and impressive

consolation : something that makes you feel better when you are unhappy

captivity : the state of being kept as a prisoner

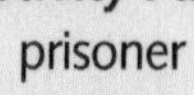

As young Prince Khurram, he commanded his father's army and led many campaigns. Although he wasn't Jahangir's eldest son, he soon became his favourite. 'Gradually, as his years increased, so did his excellence,' wrote Jahangir. He further says, 'In art, in reason, in battle there is no comparison between him and my other children.' However, in 1623 CE, he revolted against his father due to **conspiracies** against him in the royal court. He reconciled with his father in 1625 CE. On his father's death in 1627 CE, he rushed to Agra to claim the throne. After having killed some of his brothers and nephews, and others who might take the throne, he was crowned the emperor in 1628 CE.

Jahangir receiving Prince Khurram

In the first year of his reign, Shah Jahan had to face the rebellion of the Bundela chief, Jujhar Singh, who had moved into Mughal territory. He surrendered to the Mughal army initially but revolted again in 1635 CE. Later he was pursued by the Mughal troops and killed.

Another revolt that Shah Jahan faced was that of Khan Jahan Lodi in 1628 CE, who had joined forces with the ruler of Ahmednagar. Shah Jahan realized the importance of the situation and decided to personally supervise the war against Lodi. Finally, in 1630 CE, Khan Jahan had to give up. He died near the fort of Kalanjar.

The name Shah Jahan in Persian means 'the ruler of the world'. True to his name, he wanted to expand his empire. The part of South India known as the Deccan was one area where the previous Mughal kings had not been very successful.

In 1631 CE, Shah Jahan sent the Mughal army to the Deccan. At first the rulers of Golconda and Bijapur resisted, but they had to eventually surrender. Shah

Jahan did not take over the two kingdoms, but forced them to pay his kingdom money each year.

During Shah Jahan's rule, his army also forced back the Portuguese in Bengal, captured the Rajput kingdoms in the west, and marched in the north-west beyond the Khyber Pass. Under his rule, the size of army and nobles was increased four times. To maintain them, he increased taxes, which made life difficult for the peasants.

The Mughal empire reached its greatest prosperity in the reign of Shah Jahan. As an emperor he led a hard life, personally supervising the administration in detail. He appointed men of highest ability as his ministers. During his time, Lahore, Delhi, Agra and Ahmedabad became large centres of commerce and crafts and were linked by roads and waterways to distant places and ports. He was an orthodox Muslim but was not unfair to his non-Muslim subjects.

Under his rule, men of literature and fine art were respected and honoured. He **commissioned** hundreds of paintings and engravings for his palaces, which can still be seen to this day. He was himself an excellent **calligrapher**. Poetry, music, painting, dancing, astronomy, mathematics and medicine flourished under his patronage.

An example of calligraphy inside the Taj Mahal

He believed in **magnificence** and was a lover of all things big: big mosques, big forts and big gemstones. Shah Jahan built many splendid monuments. The most famous is the Taj Mahal at Agra. The Taj Mahal was built as a tomb for his wife Mumtaz Mahal, who had died at the age of thirty-nine while giving birth to their fourteenth child. It is said that her dying wish was that 'he should build a tomb in her memory such as the world had never seen before.' The heart-broken emperor decided to build the most splendid tomb in the world. Constructed in white marble, the Taj Mahal was decorated from inside with semi-precious stones. It has verses from the *Koran*, the holy book of Muslims, beautifully carved on its walls. It is truly one of the wonders of the world. Shah Jahan also built the Pearl Mosque at Agra.

Mumtaz Mahal

The Taj Mahal

He moved the capital from Agra to Delhi, which was the usual seat of Muslim power. He was the founder of the new city of Shahjahanabad, the present-day Old Delhi, which he made his capital in 1648 CE. He built the famous Lal Qila and Jama Masjid as part of Shahjahanabad. He got the fabulous Peacock Throne made for himself. It was made of solid gold and decorated with precious jewels including the Koh-i-Noor diamond.

Red Fort, Delhi

A painting showing Shah Jahan on the Peacock Throne

In September 1657 CE, Shah Jahan fell ill. The physicians were not hopeful about his recovery. As soon as the news of his illness reached his sons, they started making preparations for capturing the throne. In 1658 CE, Aurangzeb took over and imprisoned his father. Shah Jahan spent the last eight years of his life imprisoned in a part of the Agra Fort. Only Jahanara, his devoted daughter, was allowed to visit him. Yet his only **consolation** was that from his prison window he could see Taj Mahal, where his beloved wife lay buried. He died in 1666 CE in **captivity** and was buried by the side of his wife.

Did you know?

The Taj Mahal took twenty years to construct and 20,000 men were involved in its building!

Exercises

1. **Answer the following.**
   (a) How did Shah Jahan come to the Mughal throne?
   (b) Describe the Deccan campaign of Shah Jahan.
   (c) Describe the Taj Mahal built by Shah Jahan.
   (d) How was Shah Jahan treated in his last days by Aurangzeb?

2. **Fill in the blanks.**
   (a) Shah Jahan was the son of .... and the grandson of ....
   (b) Shah Jahan was called Prince .... in his early years.
   (c) In 1631 CE, Shah Jahan sent the Mughal army to capture ....
   (d) Shah Jahan was the founder of the new city of ....

3. **Say whether the following are True or False.**
   (a) Shah Jahan moved the capital from Delhi to Agra.
   (b) Lal Qila and Jama Masjid were built as part of Shahjahanabad.
   (c) Jahanara was the daughter of Aurangzeb.
   (d) The Taj Mahal was built by Shah Jahan at Delhi.
   (e) Shah Jahan was an excellent calligrapher.

Things to do

1. **For your scrapbook.**
   Find pictures of buildings and monuments built during Shah Jahan's time and paste them in your scrapbook. With the help of your teacher, write two or three sentences about each of them.

2. **Find out!**
   Find out the names of the six great Mughal Emperors. Also try to find one interesting fact about each of them.

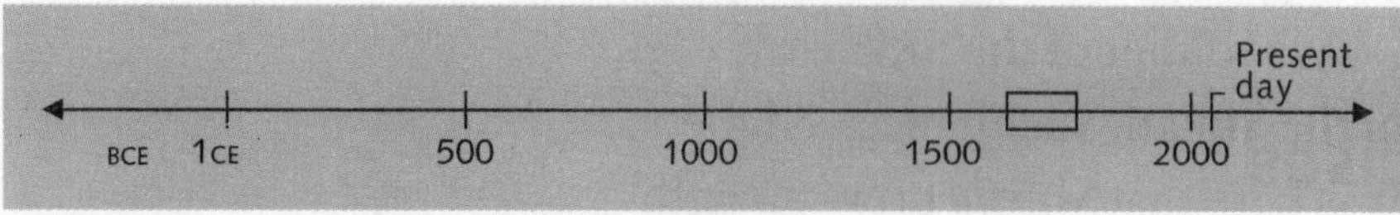

16

Shivaji
—The daring soldier

You have already read about the great Mughal emperors, Babur, Akbar and Shah Jahan. During the reign of Aurangzeb, the great-grandson of Akbar, the empire grew to its largest. The whole of North India, Central India and a part of South India were under the Mughals. It was in the Deccan that the Mughal power, for the first time, faced a challenge from the brave Maratha leader, Shivaji.

Shivaji, the founder of the last great Hindu empire in India—that of the Marathas—was born in the hill-fortress of Shivner in 1627 CE.

Shivaji

Words to remember

jagir : allotment of land with rights passed on from father to son.

treasure-train : persons, carriages and animals moving in a line carrying treasure.

ledge : narrow, horizontal shelf coming out of a cliff.

alliance : union of states by agreement.

premature : happening before the usual time.

His father, Shahji, was a soldier of the Sultan of Ahmadnagar. From the Sultan, Shahji received the **jagir** of Poona. It was here that Shivaji grew up with his mother Jija Bai and his devoted guardian and tutor, Dadaji Khonddev. Dadaji looked after Shivaji's education. He was an old soldier himself and he took care of Shivaji like a son. He taught him to ride and to shoot, and Shivaji with a band of young men of his own age, climbed the hills and explored the wild country around. Shivaji's mother was a pious Hindu lady. She told him stories from the *Ramayana* and the *Mahabharata* and Shivaji never grew tired of listening to the tales of battles and of the heroes in those great epics.

Shivaji's mother, Jijabai

Shivaji often dreamt of the day when he would be able to unite the Maratha people and set up an independent kingdom. Near Poona there was a small hill-fort called Torna. In 1646 CE, Shivaji decided to attack and capture it with his small army. One morning during the monsoon, when the commander was away, he galloped into the fort with his small band of soldiers. They captured all the arms, and more importantly, all the treasure.

Shivaji captured four other fine forts on the border of his little kingdom. Unfortunately, he had spent all his money capturing them and had now nothing left to pay his soldiers.

One day Shivaji was sitting in his fort at Kondana, thinking about the means to get some money. Suddenly, one of his officers came up the great stone steps.

'I have news,' said the officer breathlessly. 'One of our soldiers has just reported that some treasure is going to be moved from Kalyan to Bijapur.'

'We must capture it.' said Shivaji. 'The governor of Kalyan must be sending money to the Sultan of Bijapur. That is the money taken from our poor Maratha peasants. We shall try to get it back.'

Shivaji sat with his officers late into the night making plans to attack the **treasure-train**, and two days later they set out. The treasure was being carried on elephants. It had to pass through a narrow, rocky road at the side of some high hills. Well before dawn Shivaji and his men were in position. Shivaji had divided his soldiers into two groups, one on the left and the other on the right side of the road. High on the rocks above, but well out of sight of the road, Shivaji had placed twenty to thirty men. All night they had rolled up heavy rocks and stones on to a **ledge** above the gap. Everyone waited in silence.

Suddenly they heard the sound of horse's feet and elephant bells. The men on the top of the gap looked down upon the road and saw a long row of horsemen followed by elephants loaded with chests of treasure. As soon as the first few horses had entered the gap, huge rocks were rolled down on them. The horsemen in front, fearing that some soldiers were waiting for them ahead, did not known which way to turn.

It was at that moment that Shivaji's men attacked them in the rear. The attack was so sudden that the soldiers were quickly killed and the treasure carried by Shivaji to his fort.

Shivaji was now rich again and could afford to pay his soldiers. He took nine more forts of Bijapur and even attacked and captured Kalyan. The Sultan of Bijapur became very angry. He arrested Shivaji, who was then living in Bijapur, and refused to release him until Shivaji made a promise of good behaviour. Shivaji thus had to stop his attacks on Bijapur for a few years. He used this time in strengthening his position and bringing under control the many Maratha chieftains.

Aurangzeb

After some time, Shivaji again began his attacks and by 1658 CE, the whole of north Konkan was under him. At this time, Shah Jahan's son, Aurangzeb, had just come to the throne and there was no possibility of a Mughal invasion. The Sultan of Bijapur took this opportunity to try to kill Shivaji. Afzal Khan, the brother of the queen of Bijapur, was sent to do this task. When Afzal Khan arrived close to where Shivaji was camping, he sent a brahmin called Krishnaji to talk to Shivaji, and to persuade him to meet Afzal Khan. Shivaji did not trust Afzal at all, and he managed to make Krishnaji confess that Afzal Khan wanted to murder him.

Shivaji then agreed to meet Afzal Khan. He prepared himself carefully for the meeting. He put on a steel helmet and covered it with his turban. He put on a suit of strong armour beneath his tunic and hid a dagger up his sleeve. On the fingers of his left hand, he fitted sharp steel points called 'tiger-claws.'

The two commanders met in a room with only one or two attendants. Afzal Khan at once saw that Shivaji carried no sword, although he himself had his sword at his side.

'I come as a friend,' said Afzal Khan. 'I am happy to see you.' Putting out his left hand as though to embrace Shivaji round the neck, Afzal Khan struck at him with his sword. Shivaji was saved by the steel armour beneath his tunic. He quickly plunged the dagger into Afzal Khan's back and the tiger-claws into his stomach. Shivaji's soldiers immediately attacked the army of Afzal Khan, and soon overcame them.

Shivaji and Afzal Khan

The Bijapur government tried once again to defeat Shivaji but failed. In the end, the Sultan was forced to recognize Shivaji as the ruler of the entire Konkan area.

By this time Aurangzeb had settled down as the emperor. He now sent his uncle Shaista Khan to attack Shivaji. The Khan's army captured Poona and Shivaji had to retreat. But Shivaji dressed up a handful of his men to make them look like a wedding party. In this disguise they obtained permission to enter Poona, and Shivaji managed to get into the bedroom of Shaista Khan, and killed his son. The Mughal forces were completely defeated by the Marathas and the Khan barely escaped with his life.

Shivaji now was the most popular Maratha leader and in 1664 CE, he attacked Surat with four thousand soldiers. The Mughal governor was frightened. He took shelter in a castle with some of his soldiers and left the town to Shivaji. Surat was a rich city, and Shivaji and his soldiers were able to find gold and silver in plenty. They loaded the treasure on to their horses and carried it off.

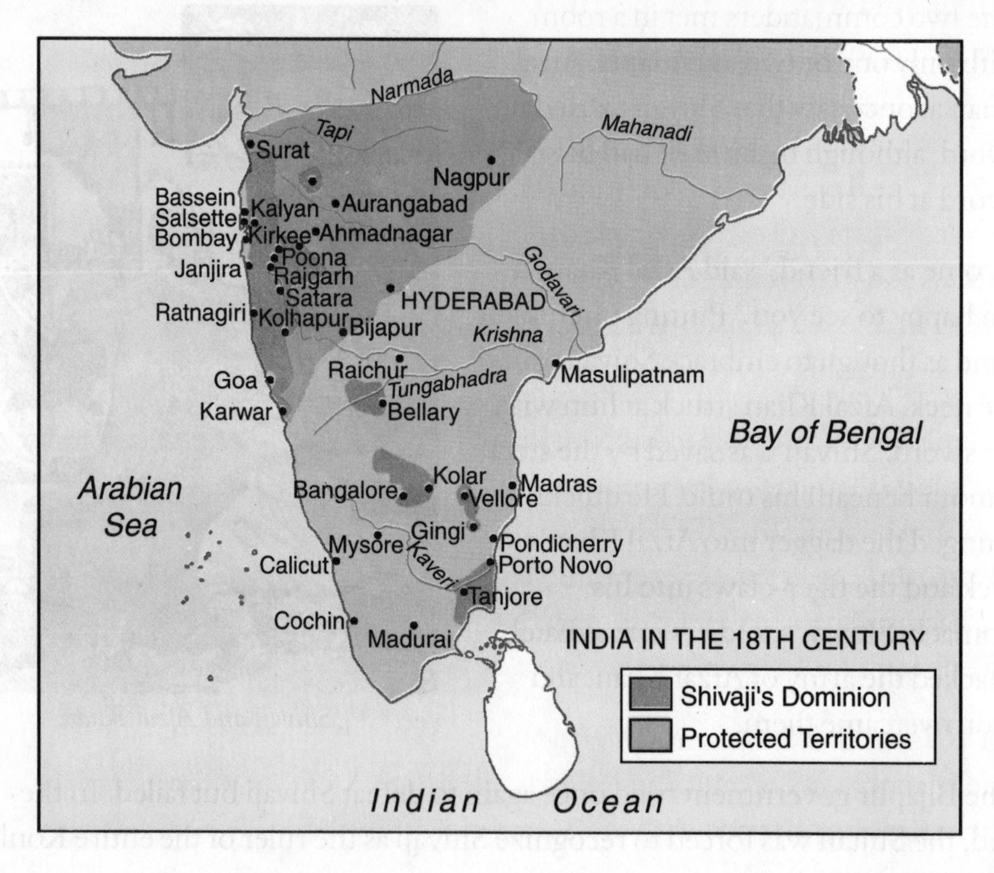

Shivaji's kingdom grew bigger and bigger. Displeased with this shameful state of affairs, Aurangzeb now sent one of his most powerful generals, Jai Singh, against Shivaji. He was told that he could go to Agra and meet the emperor for a peaceful settlement. When Shivaji came to Agra, the emperor did not want to discuss anything and instead he imprisoned Shivaji and his son, Shambhuji, almost as soon as they had arrived at his court. Shivaji did not lose heart and soon began to make plans for their escape. He began to send out large baskets of sweetmeats every day as gifts to the brahmins of Agra. One day he hid himself and his son in two of the baskets and escaped from the city. Shivaji left his son in the charge of a Maratha brahmin. He then dressed himself as a holy man and slowly made his way home through Varanasi.

Shivaji and his son were imprisoned by Aurangzeb

Did you know?

Sahar International Airport in Mumbai has been renamed Chhatrapati Shivaji International Airport in Shivaji's honour.

When Shivaji returned to his own kingdom in 1666 CE, he was received by his people with great joy. For some time, the Maratha leader kept quiet and spent his time looking after the administration. By 1670 CE, he began to recapture the forts he had given up earlier. From this time, the power of the Marathas grew steadily.

In 1674 CE, Shivaji was crowned king of the Marathas at his capital in Raigarh. He then made an **alliance** with the Sultan of Golconda, and in 1677 CE, he advanced

Shivaji's statue at Raigarh

further south and captured Vellore. Thus he became the master of a vast and powerful kingdom.

His successful career came to a close in April 1680 CE with his **premature** death at the age of fifty-three. Shivaji was not only a daring soldier and successful conqueror but also a great administrator.

Exercises

1. **Answer the following.**
   (a) Why do you think Shivaji in his early years had to make different plans to defeat the local governors?
   (b) Describe how Shivaji met Afzal Khan and killed him.
   (c) How did Shivaji drive Shaista Khan away and recapture his fort?
   (d) How did Shivaji and his son escape from Agra?
2. **Fill in the blanks.**
   (a) Shivaji was the son of .... and ....
   (b) .... looked after Shivaji's education.
   (c) The first fort that Shivaji captured was called ....
   (d) Aurangzeb sent his powerful general, ... against Shivaji.

Things to do

1. **For your scrapbook.**
   Try to find a picture of Shivaji on his horse. Cut it out and stick it in your book or draw it.
2. **Find out!**
   Find out the names of any five famous forts of India and also the names of the kings who built them.

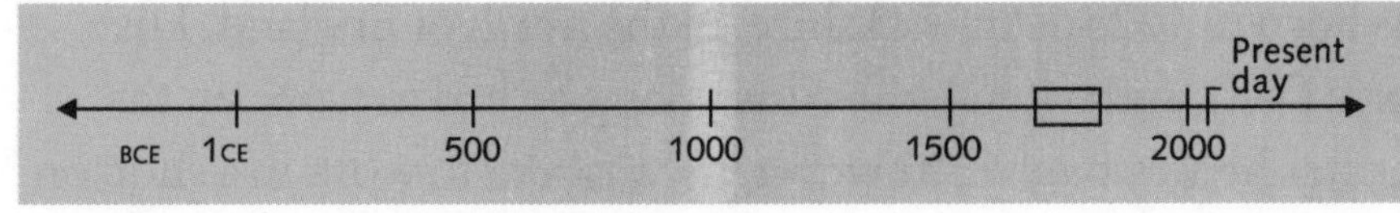

Captain James Cook 17

—The great explorer

From the time of Marco Polo, traders and explorers from many countries had made many voyages of exploration to the world yet unknown. James Cook was one of the greatest of English explorers. He discovered Australia and New Zealand. He was not only a famous explorer but also an expert at making charts. Before the voyages of Captain Cook, there were a few maps and charts showing Australia and New Zealand but the maps were not very accurate. Cook made very accurate charts on all his voyages and some of them are still used.

Captain Cook

Words to remember

mate : ship's officer below the rank of captain.
colony : a country or an area settled and controlled by people from another country, sometimes by force.
breaker : a large wave that breaks into foam as it moves towards the shore.
reef : rocks just below or above the surface of the sea.
batter : to hit somebody/something hard and repeatedly.
navigator : person who plots the course of a ship using charts.

James Cook was born in 1728 CE in Yorkshire, in the north of England. His father worked on a farm, and when James was young he had to work on the farm, too. Soon after he was twelve, however, he was sent to work in a shop on the sea coast. In Yorkshire, at that time, coal was sent by boat from the coast to other parts of England. Young James used to watch these boats in the harbour on Sundays when the shop was closed. He did not like working in the shop and after he had worked for a few years, he decided to run away. One dark Saturday evening, as soon as the shop was shut, he left quietly by the back door and ran towards the harbour. Only that morning he had seen a ship being loaded with coal and he knew it would sail early on Sunday morning.

When he got to the harbour, all the coal had been put on board. He ran up on the deck but as he put his foot on the deck, he was suddenly caught by the back of the neck.

'What are you doing here, young man?' said a fierce voice.

James was frightened by the voice, and his neck hurt; but he spoke up bravely.

'I want to see the captain.'

'I am the captain. What do you want with me?' said a fierce voice. He picked up James as though he weighed nothing, and made him sit on the railing of the ship.

'I want to work on your ship,' said James.

The captain laughed.

'You are too young,' he said.

'I am not,' said James, 'and I have been working for six years.'

Seeing how keen the young lad was, the captain gave him a job as a cabin boy. James was quick to learn and all his officers liked his work. He soon became a good seaman, and after a year or two, he joined the Navy. He rose from seaman to **mate** and was soon made Master of a British ship called the *Pembroke*. His ship went to Canada, and while he was there, he spent a great deal of time making charts of the seas he had sailed in. When he got back to England, the Navy was so pleased with him that the Government asked him to explore the Pacific Ocean. The British Government thought that there was a continent called Australia but nobody was quite sure. They felt that if they could find Australia before anyone else, they could start a colony there. This new colony would help them to become richer than the other countries. Naturally, they wanted to keep the voyage a secret.

Now it so happened that in 1769 CE, something very unusual was going to take place. The planet Venus was going to cross the sun. The Government announced, therefore, that Captain Cook was going to observe Venus, so that scientists could work out how far it was from the earth. But secretly they hoped that he would discover Australia too.

Captain Cook sailed from England in 1768 CE in a small ship called the *Endeavour*.

A long sea voyage in those days was a dangerous and difficult business. Ships were at sea for many months at a time. The ships were small but they had to

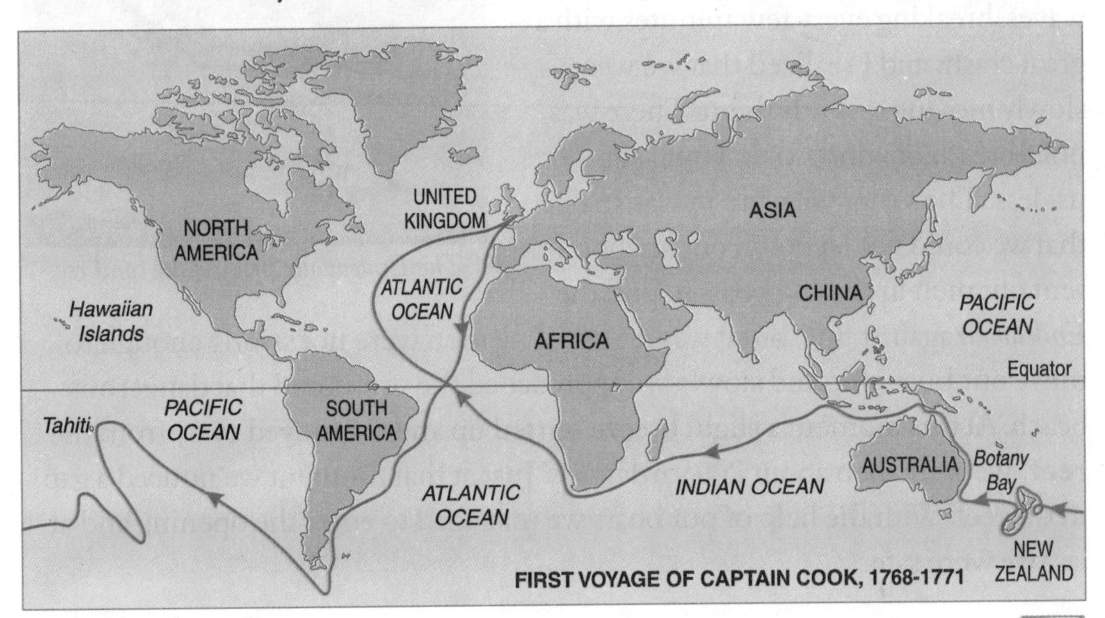

FIRST VOYAGE OF CAPTAIN COOK, 1768-1771

carry all the food and drinking water that the sailors would need on their voyages. In those days, there were no refrigerators and food went bad very easily. They could not carry vegetables or fruit, and the usual food for sailors was salt meat and biscuits. Many sailors died because the food was bad. Captain Cook was the first to think about these problems. He took with him fruits such as lemons, and he also took vegetables such as carrots; he was very careful to keep the ship spotlessly clean. In this way, he lost very few men.

The *Endeavour* came into the Pacific Ocean through the Magellan Straits in South America and then Captain Cook sailed round New Zealand and made his charts. He left New Zealand and continued west until he reached the shores of Australia. Then he travelled 2,000 miles up the Australian coast.

The voyage was an exciting one. James Cook wrote:

The Endeavour striking the coral reef

It was early morning, before dawn. We were quite near the coast and I could hear the waves roaring on the beach. As soon as it became light I could see the **breakers** about a mile away. There were huge waves, breaking every few minutes with a great crash; and I realized that we were slowly moving towards them. There was not a breath of wind, so that our sails were useless. The water we were in was so deep that we could not let down our anchor. I sent out men in rowing boats to pull the *Endeavour* against tide, but it was no use. The men were not strong enough to move our huge ship and slowly we approached the waves and that dangerous beach. At this moment a slight breeze started up and we moved away from the **reef**. We were then about 200 yards away. Just at that moment we noticed a gap in the reef. With the help of our boats we managed to enter the opening and at last we were safe.

Captain Cook sailed home and reached England after many months at sea. When he returned to England, he found that he had become famous. The Government and the Navy were pleased with his success. They soon asked him to go on another voyage to explore the Antarctic. This time he planned to go past Africa, and approach Australia from the east. He sailed down from the Cape of Good Hope into the Antarctic Sea. There was ice and snow and it was bitterly cold. Fierce gales **battered** his ship, and they were surrounded by icebergs. Captain Cook became ill and so did many of his men. Captain Cook thoroughly explored the whole area and discovered a number of new islands to the north of New Zealand. When Cook arrived home, after over three years at sea, he was promoted to the rank of a Captain at last. He published a book called *The Journals of Captain Cook*.

Captain Cook was killed in Hawaii

Captain Cook was not content to remain in England for long. He started on another long voyage in 1776 CE and arrived at Hawaii in 1778 CE. Captain Cook and his men were made welcome on the island. The Hawaiians gave them fresh food and water and allowed Captain Cook to repair his ships. In 1779 CE, they left Hawaii, but soon after that a great gale came up and destroyed the *Resolution,* one of Cook's ships. They went back to Hawaii to get it repaired. When they got there, they found that the people of Hawaii were no longer friendly. The king of the island sent some of his men out to Cook's ships and stole one of their small boats. Captain Cook went ashore to talk to the king, but while he was doing so, one of the king's men threw a spear at him which killed him instantly, and he was immediately chopped to pieces. On that spot a monument was built to remind us of the discoveries of Captain Cook.

Cook became famous by discovering Australia. He left us not only accurate charts of the countries and seas he travelled in, but also his diaries. Here is something he wrote in his diary:

> 23 June 1770
>
> I sent three men into the country to shoot pigeons. They returned with about half a dozen. One of the men saw an animal. It was the colour of a mouse, very slender and very swift. I saw one of those animals this morning. It was the size of a greyhound and shaped like one, with a very long tail. I should have taken it for a dog, but for its walking or running; it jumped like a hare or a deer. It is not at all like any other European animal I ever saw.

Did you know?

The Cook Strait separating the North Island from the South Island in New Zealand, and connecting the Tasman Sea on the west with the Pacific Ocean on the east is named after Captain James Cook.

Captain Cook is still remembered as an outstanding sea captain, a **navigator** and a maker of accurate maps.

Exercises

1. Answer the following.

(a) What were the difficulties that the sailors faced during their long voyages? How did Captain Cook try to solve them?

(b) Can you guess the name of the peculiar animal that Cook saw in Australia? This animal is still found mostly in Australia.

(c) Which countries did Captain Cook discover?

(d) Why did the British Government want to keep Cook's voyage to find Australia a secret?
(e) Can you name the different ships that have been mentioned in this chapter?
(f) How did Captain Cook die?

2. **Fill in the blanks.**
(a) Captain Cook was born in ....
(b) He was made Master of a British ship called ....
(c) Captain Cook published a book called ....
(d) A .... was built to remind us of the discoveries of Captain Cook.

3. **Say whether the following are True or False.**
(a) James Cook was one of the greatest of American explorers.
(b) Captain Cook sailed from England in 1768 CE in a small ship called the *Endeavour*.
(c) Many sailors in those days died on the ship because the food was bad.
(d) In 1769 CE, the planet Mercury was going to cross the sun.
(e) The *Endeavour* came into the Pacific Ocean through the Magellan Straits in North America.

Things to do

1. **For your scrapbook.**
Try to collect pictures of an iceberg, a whale, a seal, a penguin and a seagull.

2. **Travelling afar!**
Is there any place, city or country you would like to visit? Write six to eight lines on why you would like to travel to that place.

Unit Test 2

Maximum Marks: 15

1. Give one word for the following. ½×6=3

(a) Story of one's own life
(b) Journey for a definite purpose
(c) A military operation in which an army surrounds a place and cuts off all outside access to force surrender
(d) A person who knows the art of beautiful handwriting
(e) Union of states by agreement
(f) A country or an area settled and controlled by people from another country, sometimes by force

2. Answer the following. 1×6=6

(a) Why did Nanak give up his job?
(b) What did Paes write about Krishna Deva Raya's personality?
(c) When did Babur break all his drinking cups and vessels?
(d) Why did the Din-i- Ilahi fail?
(e) How did Shivaji and his son escape from prison?
(f) How did Captain Cook try to solve the difficulties faced by the sailors?

3. Fill in the blanks. ½×6=3

(a) The ……… is the holy book of the Sikhs.
(b) The famous painting, called *The Last Judgement*, was the work of …… .
(c) Babur was the descendant of two great Mongol leaders, Timur and …….. .
(d) Krishna Deva Raya's magnum opus is the ……… .
(e) …………built a new city called Fatehpur Sikri.
(f) Captain Cook was an expert at making………..

4. Say whether the following are True or False. ½×6=3

(a) Hampi was the capital of the Vijayanagar kingdom.
(b) Akbar was the founder of the great Mughal empire
(c) Michelangelo was very fond of going to school.
(d) Babur's army was defeated in the Battle of Panipat.
(e) Guru Nanak was the last of the ten Sikh gurus.
(f) Captain Cook died in Hawaii.